Artificial Intelligence

WILL

Revolutionize Manufacturing

by Markus Guerster

TABLE OF CONTENTS

FOREWORD

by Jeff Winter

AI is like electricity in the early 20th century – first, it was a novelty, then it became a convenience, and before long, it was indispensable. That's the journey we're on with AI in manufacturing. The book in your hands, 'Artificial Intelligence WILL Revolutionize Manufacturing' by Markus Guerster, is a continuation of this journey, delving into the transformative role of AI in reshaping the industry.

Hi there, I'm Jeff Winter. You might know me as the guy from Hitachi Solutions who turns tech talk into real talk, or as a LinkedIn Top Voice for Industry 4.0's thrilling narrative. I've spent the better part of two decades as a bridge between complex tech and the people who make our industries tick. And what a journey it's been – full of the kind of transformations that you'd expect in a great novel, except this story is real, and it's unfolding right now.

Let's talk about Industry 4.0 for a moment. It's a buzzword for sure, but one that's rich with meaning. For me, it's the best way to describe the era we are living in right now that brings together technology, data, and human ingenuity. It's more than just making things smart (our machines, processes, and decisions) – it's about completely changing the way the industry operates and provides value. And AI? It's the brainy kid who's just joined the team, ready to take us to the championship.

From my vantage point on the executive boards of MESA and ISA, an advisor to half a dozen other institutes, and in my conversations with industry leaders, I've seen the lightbulb moments when AI turns a challenge into an opportunity. It's in these stories, some of which you'll find within these pages, where the abstract becomes tangible. Whether it's AI predicting a machine's hiccup before it stalls production, or finely tuning a supply chain, these aren't just case studies; they're glimpses into the future we're shaping right now.

In the period spanning late 2022 to early 2023, the rise of consumer-facing generative AI tools marked a significant shift in how both the public and enterprises perceived AI's potential. Although discussions about generative AI's capabilities started with the introduction of GPT-2 in 2019, its full promise only became palpable to businesses recently. While AI has already been on organizations' radars, generative AI has democratized its application, allowing it to permeate every business facet. This generative wave, I believe, is pushing AI from isolated applications to being an enterprise's central nervous system.

Economic projections suggest this AI evolution could infuse the global economy with **$2.6 to $4.4 trillion** annually according to McKinsey & Company[i]. In addition, they are anticipating AI potentially bringing forward the automation of half of all work to a decade earlier than expected. Its influence on everything is undeniable.

But what about the impact in manufacturing? According to McKinsey's "The state of AI in 2023: Generative AI's breakout year," manufacturing reported the most amount of cases of cost reduction, but also the most amount of cases of revenue increases out of eight functions spanning all industries. On top of that, it has the most cases of companies reporting revenue increases of 10% or more[ii]. The power is undeniable.

As you flip through the pages of this book, you'll see how AI in manufacturing isn't just a side act, it's the main event. We're talking about augmenting human skills with a level of precision and foresight that was once the stuff of science fiction. You'll hear stories where AI didn't just improve processes; it reinvented them. It's like having a crystal ball, but instead of vague prophecies, you get clear, actionable insights.

Now, I won't promise that every anecdote will have you at the edge of your seat, but I do promise they'll have you nodding along, thinking, "Yep, I can see how that changes everything." From the subtle ways AI is becoming a co-worker on the plant floor to the big leaps forward in predictive maintenance, these stories aren't just cool tales – they're the signs of change, and they point to a road paved with opportunity.

So, welcome to the club – the innovators, the thinkers, the makers. Whether you're a seasoned pro in the world of manufacturing or just dipping your toes in, there's something here for you. This is your invitation to think big, to dream of a future where AI isn't just a tool but a teammate.

- Jeff Winter
  Industry 4.0 and AI enthusiast

INTRODUCTION

by Markus Guerster

Welcome to a story that starts in a little town in Germany, where there are more cows than people (almost!). At the age of 15, I needed some extra money. Despite the town's size, there was a local but sizeable dairy factory. So, like most people in town, I started working my summers there.

I didn't have any skills to show, so my job was simple and tough. I recall spending eight hours a day rooted to the same spot, repeating the same task endlessly. This repetitive nature of the job was grueling. I hated it, and it was physically and mentally tiring.

But at the same time, I was also amazed by the fast-moving machinery that never stopped, day or night. It sparked a curiosity in me. I kept thinking about ways to make the machines and the whole production line work better.

My mind kept envisioning how the machines could talk to each other, exchange data about their performance, and adjust speed automatically. How temperature is automatically monitored and controlled. Dashboards on big TVs inform how things are going and what issues occurred. I later came to realize these aspects fall under the term *Industry 4.0*, coined by the German government around this time.

While I had vivid ideas, I was too young to turn these ideas into reality. This was frustrating, and it really bothered me. Hence, I decided to go to college. I studied Mechanical Engineering, and soon, I was developing software and had the privilege to research on Artificial Intelligence (AI) and Machine Learning (ML) at MIT. I started with projects for satellites, but eventually, I made my way back to manufacturing.

During one of my Christmas visits back to my hometown, I had the chance to tour the dairy factory again – roughly 15 years after my summer experience working there.

Before the visit, I was thinking back to the ideas I had as a young teenager. I created a mental picture in my head of a digital, connected, and data-driven factory. Fifteen years of Industry 4.0 in Germany must have amounted to something, right? The dairy factory has been expanding ever since, capturing more market share and delivering products worldwide. So surely, it must be doing something right.

On the day of the tour, I began trying to map a mental picture of what I felt reality should be. Where are the TVs showing how the production is running? I couldn't find them. Where can I see how the current batch compares to past batches? Nowhere. I asked how workers know what product is currently being produced. I was pointed to a piece of paper.

Yes, there were traces of digital technology, but for the most part, *nothing* changed. I couldn't believe it. It had been 15 years of huge promises around Industry 4.0.

And, as it turns out, the dairy factory is not an outlier. In fact, many other manufacturers are even earlier in their digital transformation journey. The dairy factory is not a late adopter – I actually saw an above-average factory. Puzzling.

I was in deep shock. What the hell happened to Industry 4.0?

VIII

For weeks, I couldn't think of anything else. I started waking up during the night, grabbing my phone, and Googling things like: "Why is Industry 4.0 adoption slow?". None of this made sense to me.

At MIT, I researched for years on how to make AI smarter. That usually involved humongous datasets. But it all seemed meaningless when realizing that physical paper is still the predominant "data source" for some manufacturers.

It didn't feel like the typical research-to-practice gap. It appeared as two completely different worlds – separated by decades in time.

I was becoming obsessed with figuring out how to bring these two worlds together. How to bring AI to manufacturers.

And that was the triggering point for me to take action and start my own company, MontBlancAI. I saw the opportunity to make a difference in providing manufacturers with the modern tools they deserve.

It feels like coming full circle, back to the factory, but now I have a whole set of AI and ML tools to help make things better.

I wrote this book to share my perspective and leave you with a framework of actions. And, maybe, this book is doing its small part to make Industry 4.0 more real. So much so that when I tour factories in another 15 years, reality matches my mental picture more closely.

———

Even though I've worked in manufacturing for a few years, I still see myself as pretty new to this industry. This means I look at things from a new, younger point of view. Some might think my ideas are a bit naïve (and they are probably right to some degree), but one could also say they're simply fresh. I wanted to write this book early in my career to share my excitement and new ideas about AI for manufacturing before they get old. To paraphrase Bill Gates, writing helps you sort out your thoughts.

To ensure the book is realistic and practical, I talked to hundreds of experienced manufacturing leaders and experts leading up to writing this. This mix of new ideas grounded in expert knowledge gives this book a unique perspective.

I've written this book for:

- People who run manufacturing businesses, like CEOs, CTOs, COOs, and Plant Managers.

    Engineers and tech folks in manufacturing.

- Integrators and consultants who help out in manufacturing.

You don't need to know anything about AI to read this book. I've written it to be easy to get through, maybe even in one long plane ride. And there are QR codes throughout the book if you want additional and free resources to learn more about AI-related topics that interest you.

So, whether you already have a multi-year AI and Industry 4.0 strategy or you just want to learn about it, I invite you to come along as we look at how AI is changing manufacturing.

1

TOMORROW'S FACTORY

As we take a step back and observe a typical factory of an average company, we find ourselves in a setting that has only partially embraced automation. The operation is a blend of manual, semi-automated, and fully automated processes. Within these walls, a tremendous amount of data buzzes through the circuits of PLCs (Programmable Logic Controllers), capturing every second detail through an array of sensors and actuators.

This data is often displayed in real-time on HMI (Human-Machine Interface) panels and might also be fed to some SCADA (Supervisory Control and Data Acquisition) servers. Yet, surprisingly, this wealth of information rarely finds its way to a centralized repository equipped for big data analytics. And even on the rare occasions when it is collected, it seldom is leveraged to extract actionable insights.

In some corners of the factory, you might even spot employees engaged in a ritual as old as industry itself: taking manual measurements every hour and recording them on paper. They plot these points diligently, later connecting them to visualize trends over time.

Now, this might prompt the question: "What's so problematic about this traditional approach?" Well, let's consider a scenario. You receive a phone call from a customer who's disappointed with a defective batch of products. Besides the immediate customer service firefighting – reassuring the customer, organizing replacements, and the like – there's the pressing issue of preventing such failures in the future.

You make calls across your team, trying to stitch together memories and scattered data, hoping to identify the problem. But let's be honest: this approach is not a matter of minutes or hours, but more likely days or weeks. The crux of your problem lies in the disorganization of data – a labyrinth of disconnected systems that might kindly be termed "data silos" or more bluntly, "a data mess."

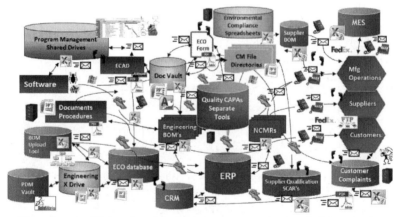

Figure 1: a simplified version of the data mess many organizations find themselves [1]

The illustration in Figure 1 succinctly captures the chaos.

When shown to different individuals across various organizations, the response is strikingly uniform. No one denies the resemblance; in fact, most agree it's a generous simplification of the situation they're entangled in. And this realization isn't confined to those in IT; from the shop floor to the executive suite, the acknowledgment of their data disorder is unanimous.So, even with the best detective work through this "data mess," you might, at best, pinpoint a root cause. But how do you prevent future occurrences? That's a whole different challenge, especially if variables change or there's a turnover in personnel.

Imagine, then, equipping your team with a system that not only expedites troubleshooting but also anticipates and resolves problems before they escalate. Such a system, leveraging real-time data, would enable decisions to be made with swiftness, enhancing production flow and reducing costly downtime. It would ensure that potential issues are promptly addressed, upholding quality and customer satisfaction. This isn't just about maintaining the status quo; it's about fostering a culture of continuous improvement and operational excellence.

In a fully integrated system, the end-to-end material flow of factories could be augmented. An optimized production plan can be generated for your customers' orders based on tank level, machine capabilities, warehouse capacity, and staff availability. Raw ingredients and spare parts can be reordered automatically and delivered just in time.

Now, consider the strategic advantage of adopting such advanced systems. Artificial Intelligence (AI) is not about replacing human expertise but augmenting it. In a landscape where manufacturers are differentiated by their willingness to embrace innovation and cut cost, those who integrate AI into their operations are poised to lead. The question then becomes, on which side of this technological divide do you envision your business? The choice is between adhering to traditional methods or progressing toward a future where smart factories are the norm.

This pivotal moment is not arbitrary. The convergence of technological advancements has created a unique opportunity for industries to transform. The tools and systems necessary for this evolution are now within reach. It's an ideal time to transition from the conventional factory settings of today to the intelligent, data-driven factories of tomorrow.

If the prospect of tapping into the latent potential within your data resonates with you, then the insights offered in the remainder of this book are valuable to you. They are designed to guide you in capturing this potential.

Moreover, if you find that the strategies outlined here do not shed new light on your operations or provide actionable insights, I am committed to not only refunding your purchase but also supplying additional resources to ensure you have the means to explore alternative solutions.

The future is here, and it's time to decide where you stand in the dawning era of smart manufacturing.

2

WHAT HAPPENED TO INDUSTRY 4.0?

The term Industry 4.0 is over a decade old. The German Federal Ministry for Economic Affairs and Climate Action and the Federal Ministry of Education and Research define Industry 4.0 as: "the intelligent networking of machines and processes for industry with the help of information and communication technology." A practical example of this would be, "Screws communicating with assembly robots, self-driving forklifts stocking high shelves with goods, intelligent machines coordinating independently-running production processes – people, machines, and products are directly connected with each other: the fourth industrial revolution has begun." [2]

Industry 4.0 has countless related concepts and derived definitions like IIoT, IoT, AIoT, Big Data, Cloud computing, Virtual Reality, Smart Manufacturing, Intelligent Factory, Digital Transformation, etc., and promises a revolution in how we craft and create.

Diving into the subject, I've sifted through article after article, trying to piece together the real use-cases and value propositions of Industry 4.0 in manufacturing. What I found was more of a mosaic than a clear picture. I even put together a word cloud from these readings, expecting to see a pattern emerge.

Figure 2: word cloud summarizing countless Industry 4.0 articles [3,4,5,6,7,8,9,10,11,12,13,14,15]

Yet, there's no single term dominating the landscape. It's a scattering of ideas, each pointing to a different part of the puzzle, with no single piece revealing what Industry 4.0 is actually about (or whichever other term you might want to use).

Adding complexity to the mix, the effectiveness of Industry 4.0 varies widely based on where a factory is, how much it costs to run, what it's making, and how much profit it's pulling in. It's tough to nail down what's most important for each factory or even what success looks like.

Let's look at a few examples from case studies to illustrate the diversity in results.

Take, for example, Oyak Cement, which holds five public cement companies amongst others. Electricity accounts for 80% of their cost. Just a 1% decrease in energy usage results in millions in annual savings. They leveraged Industry 4.0 to specifically focus on optimizing their operations for energy consumption. [16]

Another example within the same industry is Votorantim Cimentos. Optimizing energy consumption was important to the company, but the more pressing issue was to reduce their high maintenance cost. By becoming more predictive, Votorantim was able to reduce its maintenance cost by 10%. [17]

Unscheduled downtime and hard-to-predict throughput were issues that New Belgium Brewing faced. They implemented Industry 4.0 solutions to get insights into their real-time data, which eventually led to improvements in their OEE. [18]

Staying within the same industry, Deschutes Brewery used real-time data completely differently. They suffered from unexplainable temperature spikes. With the proper Industry

4.0 tooling in place, their team was able to identify the root cause and hold off from capital expenditure.

Another brewery, Heineken, is using Industry 4.0 to make data-driven decisions around its sustainability goals by collecting and analyzing water and CO_2 consumption across plants. [19]

Henkel, the pharma giant, uses Industry 4.0 with similar goals to drive sustainability. However, their challenge was to collect and communicate consumption and emission data across the supply chain. [20]

Another pharma company, Pfizer, is also suffering from data silos, but in their drug discovery division. By leveraging Industry 4.0, they established a single truth and enabled a higher level of collaboration across teams. [21]

I could continue with numerous additional examples, but I think you get the idea. If you look back over the examples and try to identify a common pattern, it looks pretty much like the word-cloud. It's diverse how Industry 4.0 is used across industries and even across companies of similar size within the same industry.

My point is: what if we stopped trying to label everything so precisely? Can we find a common denominator across these use cases?

There might be a more straightforward approach. I'm talking about cutting through the noise to focus on *what actions we can take* —concentrate on the practical steps that can be taken, steps that are sure to bring some benefit. The exact value that comes from these steps will look different for everyone, given the endless variables at play. Yet, the core ideas, the basic steps – they're solid for anyone. They are *fundamental principles*.

By boiling it down to the basics and concentrating on practical measures, we can discern a path that, because of its simplicity, is universally applicable and fundamentally solid. Indeed, when viewed from this perspective, the seemingly convoluted and technical concepts of Industry 4.0 crystallize into four clear steps that every company undergoes in its journey toward achieving this industrial milestone.

The Beehive

Consider a factory akin to a bustling beehive, where each worker bee contributes to the production of honey. In this analogy, the "honey" of modern manufacturing results from numerous intelligent decisions, guided by AI in the role of an expert beekeeper.

The first step in this process is akin to the beekeeper collecting pollen, or in manufacturing terms, data collection. This involves gathering detailed information about everything happening on the shop floor, from the production rates to machine temperature readings.

Next comes the equivalent of showing where each bee is and what it's doing, or data visualization in manufacturing. This stage transforms the collected data into easily comprehensible graphs and charts, providing a clear visual representation of the factory's operations.

However, merely knowing the current state is just a start. The next step is predictions, forecasting future scenarios similar to weather predictions but in the context of manufacturing. This anticipatory approach helps in planning ahead of time and ordering material before the need becomes critical; or allows the detection of quality issues early in the process before they land at the customers' door.

The final stage involves recommendations, where actionable measures are suggested, be it tweaking a recipe or adjusting a machine's settings. These suggestions culminate in insights akin to a map guiding to the best sources of pollen, which are then disseminated across all facets of the factory, from operations to quality assurance and management.

But the process doesn't end there. It's an ongoing cycle of agile iterations, a loop of continuous learning and improvement. Each cycle informs and defines new objectives based on the insights gained from the previous one, enhancing the factory's efficiency and intelligence.

The Four Steps

Now, let's go back to the seven case studies I briefly summarized before, keeping these four steps in mind: 1) Collecting Data, 2) Communicating Data, 3) Predicting and Detecting, and 4) Recommending and Acting.

1. Collecting Data. In all case studies, collecting (real-time) data is the fundamental first step. Oyak Cement needed to gather more detailed data about their energy usage and the causing factors. Votorantim Cimentos had to monitor their equipment to enable maintenance solutions.

2. Communicating Data. The data collected is only as good as its interpretation, which is why visualization is crucial. For New Belgium Brewing, visualizing their operations in real-time allowed them to spot inefficiencies and enhance Overall Equipment Effectiveness (OEE). Deschutes Brewery could pinpoint temperature anomalies through clear visualization tools, averting unnecessary expenditure.

3. Predicting and Detecting. Once you have a clear visualization, the next logical step is to use this data to predict future outcomes. Heineken uses predictive analytics to forecast their water and CO2 consumption, which helps in planning sustainable operations. Votorantim Cimentos, through predictive maintenance models, anticipates machinery failures, preventing costly downtimes and maintenance.

4. Recommending and Acting. The final step is taking informed actions based on the insights gained. Henkel's and Pfizer's cases illustrate this well. Henkel applied their data insights to drive sustainability initiatives across their supply chain, while Pfizer tackled the challenge of data silos in drug discovery by creating a unified platform for collaboration, thereby accelerating their research and development process.

By examining these seven case studies, we can see a pattern of how companies, despite operating in different sectors or facing varied challenges, employ the same core steps of Industry 4.0 to drive innovation and efficiency.

Let's look at another case study that traverses all four steps:

Back in 2019, the Wuxi factory operated by Bosch Automotive Diesel System Co. Ltd. experienced a surge in demand triggered by regulatory changes in emissions control. [22] The factory turned to Industry 4.0. Here's how the factory exemplified the four steps:

The factory harnessed the power of RFID and embedded sensors to collect vast amounts of real-time data. This critical first step laid the groundwork for a transformative shift, enabling the factory to capture a digital snapshot of its operational heartbeat.

With data in hand, the factory employed sophisticated tools to translate raw information into actionable insights. Visualization of production data allowed for a clear, comprehensive view of the manufacturing landscape, empowering decision-makers with the clarity needed to address inefficiencies and streamline operations.

The Wuxi factory didn't just stop at understanding the present; it looked forward. By analyzing patterns and trends within the data, the factory developed predictive models to forecast potential disruptions, ensuring that preemptive measures could be taken to maintain a steady production flow.

The final, critical step involved putting these insights into action. The predictive analytics allowed for proactive management of the production line, minimizing downtime, and ensuring that the factory could meet the increased demand without compromising on efficiency or quality.

Key Takeaways

Industry 4.0 has been an aspirational vision for decades, promising a revolution in manufacturing through advanced technologies like IoT, Big Data, Cloud Computing, and more. Yet, as we've explored in this chapter, the reality on the ground is far more nuanced. The journey towards this revolution is not uniform; it varies widely based on individual factory circumstances, resources, and strategic goals.

Here are the key takeaways:

- **Industry 4.0 is not one-size-fits-all:** It's a set of tools and methodologies that can be adapted to a company's unique needs and challenges.
- **Data is foundational:** Without quality data collection processes in place, the rest of the Industry 4.0 transformation cannot follow.
- **Visualization is key:** Data needs to be presented in a way that's easily understandable to facilitate quick and accurate decision-making.
- **Predictive analytics are transformative:** They empower businesses to move from reactive to proactive, anticipating problems before they occur.
- **Action is the final and crucial step:** Insights are only as valuable as the actions they prompt. The real power of Industry 4.0 is in its ability to drive smarter, faster, and more effective operational decisions.

As we look toward the future of manufacturing, it's clear that the principles of Industry 4.0 will continue to evolve and shape the industry. The challenge lies in cutting through the noise to focus on the fundamental steps that drive value, regardless of the specific technology or terminology used. This chapter's exploration into diverse applications of Industry 4.0 underscores a universal truth: it's not about chasing labels but about finding practical, actionable pathways to improvement and innovation in the complex tapestry of modern manufacturing.

As we transition from the foundational understanding of Industry 4.0's landscape to the mechanics of its implementation, we pivot towards a compelling framework: *The Flywheel behind Industry 4.0*. In the upcoming chapter, we will dissect this concept and integrate the four pivotal steps – Collect Data, Communicate Data, Predict and Detect, and Recommend and Act into a coherent framework.

3

THE INDUSTRY 4.0 FLYWHEEL

In our journey through the realms of Industry 4.0, we have encountered various facets of its application across diverse industries. Now, we converge these insights into a dynamic, cyclical process I refer to as "The Flywheel behind Industry 4.0." This concept encapsulates the essence of Industry 4.0, transforming it from a set of isolated initiatives into a self-sustaining cycle of continuous improvement and innovation. The flywheel comprises four crucial steps, each feeding into the next, creating momentum that propels the entire manufacturing process forward:

Collecting Data: This initial step involves gathering comprehensive operational data. From machine performance metrics to production timelines, every piece of data acts as a vital cog in the flywheel, setting the stage for informed decision-making.

Communicating Data: Next, we translate the amassed data into an easily comprehensible visual format. This step is crucial as it transforms abstract numbers into actionable intelligence, allowing decision-makers to perceive patterns, inefficiencies, and opportunities with clarity.

Predicting and Detecting: Leveraging the power of machine learning, we forecast future needs, trends, and potential challenges. This predictive capability enables proactive rather than reactive strategies, aligning resources with anticipated requirements.

Recommending and Acting: The culmination of this process is implementing AI-driven suggestions for optimization and improvement. These actions are informed by the insights gained from the previous steps, ensuring that each decision is data-driven and targeted toward enhancing operational efficiency.

The Industry 4.0 Flywheel

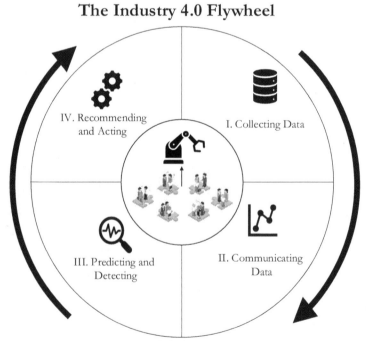

Figure 3: The Industry 4.0 Flywheel

At first glance, these steps might seem too obvious or simplistic, prompting thoughts like, "Is that really all there is to it?" However, this clarity is precisely the result of distilling the essentials, cutting through the noise to reveal the straightforward core of Industry 4.0.

But why organize these four steps into a flywheel?

The Flywheel Concept

The flywheel effect in a business context occurs when incremental progress accumulates over time, creating momentum that fuels growth. There is a direct analogy with the mechanical flywheel that stores momentum. The heavier a flywheel, the harder it is to get it started. Think about what it took to start a steam engine, with operators first needing to spin up a gigantic flywheel before engaging the engine.

If you are trying to start an Industry 4.0 effort within your organization but structure it such that the flywheel is heavy, it will require enormous resources to get things moving. And you might get frustrated and lose support before you're able to even turn the wheel once. And the thing with Industry 4.0 is that it requires at least one rotation of the flywheel, often multiple rotations, until momentum is generated and you can see value and insights emerge.

And believe me, starting MontBlancAI from scratch felt (and often still does) a lot like trying to turn an impossibly heavy flywheel with bare hands. In the beginning, there were only a few hands, no money, and no tooling to help. The only thing that could be done was to figure out how to make the flywheel as small as possible and make it spin a few times.

Hence, the goal should be to *find the lightest possible flywheel* within your organization and start turning it. The rest will come naturally; you will achieve organic adoption. The wheel will spin faster and faster, the word will spread, people will *want* to get on board, and you will see significant ROI emerge.

But what happens if you stop propelling the flywheel?

It will lose momentum over time (as there is no perpetuum mobile). Industry 4.0 is not something to achieve but a continuous repetition of going through the iterations over and over again. New machines require new data connection, which, in turn, require updated predictions and recommendations. Organizational restructuring implies thinking about the escalation's phases in a new way. New products will require reconfiguration of your production lines. The good news is that keeping a well-oiled flywheel spinning is little effort compared to making it spin in the first place.

This iterative process encompasses the essence of the Industry 4.0 revolution. It's not merely about adopting new technologies but about creating a rhythmic flow of data-driven strategies that evolve and adapt with each cycle. The flywheel model underscores the importance of agility and continuous learning within the manufacturing sector, highlighting that the journey towards Industry 4.0 is not a one-time effort but a perpetual process of growth and refinement.

3.1 The Flywheel Works for Manual Processes

As someone passionate about technology, it is easy for me to overlook that new and better technology is not always the answer. While developing the Flywheel framework, I considered the four steps to be mostly driven by technology. Data is collected automatically by software. Data is visualized and predicted by software.

That changed when I found myself one Monday night working on the book and looking at a book next to me that I read a while ago – *The Goal* by Eliyahu M. Goldratt, written in 1992 [23]. Back then, technology existed, but not to the extent it does today. I started thinking if the flywheel would also work without software (or with less of it).

So, I revisited this chapter, looked at all four steps, and realized, yes, absolutely. Even if all steps are manual and on paper, the wheel will still turn.

Collecting data can be done manually. Workers can walk around the factory, manually read temperature sensors, and write the value on a piece of paper.

You might even add these data points directly to a graph and connect them by the end of the day. You will end up with the second step, visualizing your data.

If you repeat that process over a couple of days and overlay these lines, you are able to create a (mental) prediction of what the temperature should look like throughout the day. For example, we humans do this automatically when it comes to the outside temperature over the summer during a window of sunny weather. And for sure, we will notice when the temperature suddenly drops for a day and it starts to rain. That's the anomaly detection part. We've created a mental model of how we predict the day to be, and if it doesn't fit the model, we say to ourselves, "Something is off here."

A 10-degree Celsius (or 50-degree Fahrenheit) day feels like an outlier during the summer when we are used to 20-degree Celsius (or 70-degree Fahrenheit) as we expected it to be warmer. And the opposite is true for the winter months.

Another example is when an experienced worker learned over decades what healthy machines sound like. He or she can immediately detect when something is off. They build a prediction of what it should sound like and identify an anomaly when it is different.

And then the action part – the experienced worker might be training another worker on the job. So, instead of performing the corrective action themselves, they *recommend* an action for the person in training to perform. Or they *act* and fix the issue themselves directly.

All of this led me to the idea that the flywheel is based on fundamental principles as each of these steps can be performed manually or automatically. It is easy to see how technological advancements have helped us spin the wheel easier and faster. Image the cost per measurement when somebody needs to physically go around and note down the value vs. an automated data collector.

Having a framework that allows for steps to be interchangeable between manual and automatic comes with great flexibility. You can "sprinkle in" technology over time and automate the steps that are most important to you.

3.2   How to Measure ROI

While I'll make the argument later that getting started with Industry 4.0 is cheaper than you might think (thanks to AI), there are still resources (time, money, political capital, etc. ...) that need to be allocated to such an effort. You might ask how you should measure the Return on Investment (ROI). What does success look like?

If you are reading this book, you most likely are in the early days of Industry 4.0 adoption. You might want to learn more about it, or maybe you have started a few smaller projects here and there. You might already have data collected in a data lake but don't really know how this can be useful. If that is you, then you are in what I call Phase 1.

In most instances, ROI is calculated based on monetary measurements like boosting revenue, increasing profits, or reducing costs. Having digested plenty of case studies and talking to countless experts, it turns out that, in most cases, it is simply too far-fetched to translate the early success that has been achieved into monetary terms. Yes, you will find monetary ROI numbers (or an odd round percentage number) in some case studies, but is that really the core of what you want to achieve in these early days? There are exceptions, but my argument here is to *focus on learning* when thinking about ROI in this initial Phase 1.

Consider the analogy with a startup. The stages of a startup can be roughly divided into two phases: 1) "figuring things out" and 2) "scale what you have figured out."

In the first phase, the investor will not measure the startup on revenue and profits simply because there is none. The founders will be measured on what they figure out, what they learn about the market, and the fit of their product within the market.

You might have heard of "pivoting." That's just short for going down a path and figuring out that things don't work out. The startup needs to backtrack to square one, and it can feel like zero progress has been made. Well, except that the company *learned* something. It learned what *not* to do – which sometimes is more valuable than learning what to do. The key to survival is to be able to do enough of these iterations and learn quickly enough before the startup runs out of money.

While the startup can be strategic about which paths to go down, there is a lot of noise, uncertainty, and randomness, so focusing on keeping the flywheel small and increasing the rate of learning will inevitably increase the chances of survival.

Once "things are figured out," Phase 2 starts. It's time to scale up the business. The monetary ROI becomes increasingly what the investor will measure the startup on.

Consider as an example Kellogg's. They implemented a data collection and visualization system with the goal to understand in more depth their production processes. Through that process, they realized and *learned* that their HVAC system was using unnecessary energy to heat water that was being cooled afterward. Kellogg's then *acted* and updated the control units to balance their HVAC, resulting in USD 350,000 in annual savings.

If the Kellogg's management had measured its Phase 1 efforts with a monetary ROI associated with the improvement of production, the project could have been considered a failure. However, when measured in terms of learning, the project was a tremendous success as they learned about their HVAC inefficiencies.

With these insights, they went into Phase 2 on HVAC and were able to make a traditional business case with ROI calculation around the cost of upgrading the control units vs. the expected savings.

And that's how Industry 4.0 adoption within an organization will be most successful.

Phase 1: Focus on Learning. When starting from scratch, the ROI should be the *rate of learning*. Find that smallest flywheel and make it spin. Get people excited about the vision and celebrate failures as the most insightful learnings. Once momentum is built, transition into Phase 2.

Phase 2: Earn the Rewards. Once you have "things figured out," you can focus on the most valuable areas of Industry 4.0 for your business. You will have enough experience to clearly articulate and measure the *monetary* ROI. You will see the impact of your previous investments reflected on your bottom line.

3.2.1   Phase 1 – Focus on Learning

The journey of adopting Industry 4.0 in your business may appear daunting and expensive. This perception is common among many companies I've interacted with. Given its status as a high-tech, hyped technology frequently headlining news for its high-cost talent and scarcity, this viewpoint is understandable. Often, it seems like only large corporations with deep pockets can afford to build a team of experts with salaries alone running into millions annually for only a few heads.

For smaller companies, these figures are intimidating. Adding to this, the novelty of Industry 4.0 and the yet-to-be firmly established monetary ROI makes it challenging to justify such a massive capital expenditure upfront. But what if there's a way to start with Industry 4.0 at a very low cost or even for free?

This isn't just hypothetical. Let me give you an analogy:

Take office software as an example. Imagine the cost and effort of developing your own email messaging service. It would be prohibitively expensive, and the end product would likely fall short of what's available for a few dollars a month or even for free. Moreover, self-developed systems require ongoing maintenance, security updates, management of servers, and more. It simply doesn't make economic sense.

So, what are you doing instead? Within seconds, you can sign up for an email account and have access to a product that would have cost tens of millions to develop. At best, it's for free, and at worst, it'll cost you a few dollars every month.

And if you need to scale the solution to a whole organization? You don't need to buy servers and worry about running out of hard disk space. You just go online and add users. It's as simple as that.

Another example is ChatGPT from OpenAI. They literally spend billions of dollars on developing a product that is now accessible for free. Before OpenAI, if you wanted to have Generative AI capabilities for your company, you had to spend millions of dollars hiring a team of experts and training the model. These days are over. And given the speed of advancement, we will see even more AI-enabled products become available in the near term.

This is also true when it comes to Industry 4.0. Startups and companies absorb the capital expenditure and the complexity of development, offering plug-and-play, subscription-based solutions. This model creates a win-win situation. Manufacturers can access products they couldn't develop in-house without incurring enormous costs. They can start easily and opt out if it doesn't suit their needs.

It also solves a couple of other hindering points I commonly come across.

What is the ROI of Industry 4.0 for manufacturing?

As we have discussed in the previous chapter, there are simply too many variables at play to be able to predict a monetary ROI precisely for Phase 1 projects. There are too many uncertain factors. Instead, my argument is that you should focus on the *rate of learning*.

However, the good news is the cost of experimentation has never been so low. Many vendors provide at least trial versions for free. When calculating the ROI of something that is basically free, the hurdle of proving value suddenly becomes much smaller (I know there are always internal costs associated even if the product is free, but compare that to the millions it would cost you otherwise).

In fact, my recommendation for this Phase 1 is to embrace a *culture of learning and experimentation.* At worst, you spend a couple of hours of your and your team's time learning about if and how Industry 4.0 (and AI by extension) can be used in your factory. Not the worst outcome, is it?

But wait, how can I plan without knowing where things are heading?

By now, I hope I've convinced you that getting started with Industry 4.0 is cheaper than you thought. You might say, okay, but I still need to have a plan. How do I roll this out throughout my factory and then companywide? What is the timeline for this? And what are the resources required?

Let's get some inspiration from how software is developed today. Almost all software companies globally have shifted from a waterfall method to some sort of agile, iteration-based approach.

In the waterfall method, the complete project is planned out precisely, with detailed deadlines for years in advance. You can guess how often the project exactly followed the initial plan.

In software development, just as in manufacturing, you're dealing with complicated systems where the outcomes aren't always clear, people and organizational structures play a huge role, and it's nearly impossible to predict exactly how things will turn out.

In software development, for instance, you never know for sure how users will interact with a new feature or what creative ways they'll find to break your system. Similarly, with Industry 4.0, it's tough to foresee how workers will adapt to new technologies, how the overall organization might need to change, or what insights you'll gain from new data.

Therefore, the agile approach has seen widespread adoption. It doesn't imply to forget about planning. Planning is important, but it focuses on iterations of planning, execution, and receiving real-world feedback. These iterations are typically not more than a few weeks.

Hence, the goal of planning how to implement Industry 4.0 shouldn't be to predict every turn but to *navigate the journey with adaptability and insight*. It's about shifting the focus from defining to doing, from rigid planning to flexible thinking. This allows for rapid adjustments and pivots based on real-world feedback, ensuring that the strategy evolves with the practical needs and discoveries made along the way.

3.2.2 Phase 2 – Earn the Rewards

After successfully navigating the initial phase of Industry 4.0 implementation, where the focus was predominantly on learning and experimentation, we transition into Phase 2 – Earn the Rewards. This phase represents the maturation of your Industry 4.0 journey, where the insights and experiences gleaned from Phase 1 are leveraged to generate tangible, measurable benefits.

Understanding the Shift to Phase 2

Phase 2 is characterized by a shift in focus from exploratory learning to strategic application and optimization. The foundational work done in Phase 1 – establishing data collection processes, trialing different approaches, and understanding the capabilities and limitations of Industry 4.0 technologies – now serves as the springboard for more targeted and monetary ROI-driven initiatives.

Strategic Implementation and ROI Focus

Prioritized Investment Areas: Having experimented and learned in Phase 1, you now have a clearer understanding of which Industry 4.0 initiatives hold the most promise for your organization. This could be in the form of specific technologies, processes, or areas of operation where Industry 4.0 can deliver the highest return.

Data-Driven Decision Making: The data collected and analyzed in Phase 1 becomes a powerful tool for making informed decisions. By now, your organization should have a robust framework for utilizing this data to drive operational improvements, quality enhancements, and cost reductions.

Scaling and Integration: With proven concepts and a deeper understanding of the practical applications of Industry 4.0, it's time to scale these solutions across different departments, production lines, and plants. Integration of these technologies into everyday operations is key to maximizing their impact.

Continued Innovation and Adaptation

The success in Phase 2 is primarily measured in monetary terms - increased revenue, cost savings, improved efficiency, and return on investment. However, it's crucial to maintain a balanced view that also considers non-monetary benefits such as improved employee engagement, customer satisfaction, and brand reputation.

Even as the focus in Phase 2 is on earning rewards, it's important to maintain a mindset of continuous innovation. The landscape of Industry 4.0 is ever-evolving, and staying ahead requires ongoing adaptation and willingness to explore new technologies and methodologies.

Putting it All Together

Phase 2 of your Industry 4.0 journey is about capitalizing on the groundwork laid in Phase 1. It's a phase where strategic implementation, driven by data and insights, leads to significant operational improvements and measurable returns on investment. As you navigate this phase, remember that the journey of Industry 4.0 is cyclical – the learning and insights gained here will feed back into the flywheel, driving continuous improvement and innovation.

3.3 The Role of AI in Industry 4.0

It's time to address the pivotal role of Artificial Intelligence (AI). While we have been focusing on the structural framework of Industry 4.0, AI serves as the central enabler, enhancing and accelerating each step of this journey. Think about AI as the latest advancement in automation technology.

AI is not just a component of Industry 4.0; it's a catalyst that amplifies its impact. In the context of the four steps of our flywheel, AI plays a crucial role in each:

In Data Collection: AI enhances the ability to gather and process vast amounts of data efficiently. From intelligent sensors to automated data aggregation systems, AI-driven tools can sift through the noise to capture relevant operational data.

In Data Communication: AI algorithms can transform complex data sets into intuitive, actionable visualizations. This goes beyond traditional charts and graphs, employing sophisticated techniques like predictive analytics dashboards and real-time performance trackers.

In Predicting and Detecting: Perhaps AI's most profound impact is in its predictive capabilities. Machine Learning, a subset of AI, allows for the analysis of historical data to forecast future trends, identify potential disruptions, and suggest preventative measures.

In Recommending and Acting: AI's ability to analyze data and provide insights paves the way for smarter decision-making. It enables automated systems to make real-time adjustments in processes, enhancing efficiency and reducing human error.

Before we can dive deeper into how AI interplays with the steps of the Industry 4.0 Flywheel, a foundational understanding of AI is essential. In the next chapter, "All You Need to Know About AI," I will demystify AI, explaining its core principles and functionalities in a manner that is both comprehensive and accessible to anyone.

4

ALL YOU NEED TO KNOW ABOUT AI

In this chapter, I aim to strip away the veil of complexity that often shrouds AI, breaking it down into its fundamental components. The content here is crafted to be accessible, steering clear of technical jargon and assuming no prior knowledge of the field. I chose simplicity over technical accuracy.

For those well-versed in AI, this chapter might serve as a quick refresher. For newcomers, the concepts and terminology introduced are essential to grasp the subsequent discussions on AI's transformative value in the manufacturing sector.

A word of caution, though: AI is a broad and rapidly advancing field. It's almost certain that some aspects may not be covered here, and there's a high chance that by the time you're reading this, new developments will have emerged. AI doesn't stand still, and neither should our understanding of it. For that reason, I created a list of additional resources on AI that complement this Chapter and is kept up to date:

QR Code 1: Additional reading material on AI

Before delving into what AI is, it's often more enlightening to clarify what AI is not.

4.1   What AI is NOT

AI Lacks Sentience and Consciousness: At its core, AI is a collection of algorithms and code designed to process data. Contrary to some perceptions, AI does not possess self-awareness or emotions. It functions based on the parameters set by its creators, devoid of any form of consciousness.

AI is Not Infallible: A common misconception is that AI is perfect. However, AI systems can and do make mistakes. Just try a quick session with tools like ChatGPT in your area of expertise to understand their limitations. The reliability of AI varies; some approaches are more robust than others, but all exhibit some level of non-deterministic behavior.

AI Isn't a Cure-All Solution: While AI offers numerous benefits, it's not the answer to every problem. In some cases, simpler methods like control loops or statistical formulas are more effective. AI is a tool, advantageous in specific contexts but not universally applicable.

AI Doesn't Equate to Loss of Human Control: The notion that AI could lead to a future where humans lose control is a misunderstanding. AI is created, controlled, monitored, and maintained by humans through code and hardware. It operates within the bounds set by humans.

AI Will Not Replace Humans Entirely: AI is a powerful tool, but it is not a replacement for human capabilities. Instead, it augments human efforts. Much like a gardener with a shovel works more efficiently than one using bare hands, humans leveraging AI can outperform those who don't. However, this doesn't imply that AI will render human roles obsolete; it is an intelligent augmentation.

4.2   History of AI

To truly appreciate the potential of AI in transforming today's factories, we must first understand its roots. AI is not a recent phenomenon; it has an interesting history that stretches back decades.

The Dawn of Computational Thought: The journey begins with Alan Turing, a name synonymous with the origins of computing. In 1936, Turing envisioned a machine that could perform any conceivable mathematical computation given enough time and memory. This theoretical framework, known as the Turing machine, became the cornerstone of modern computing and, by extension, artificial intelligence. Turing's work posed the profound question: Could machines think?

The Birth of an Academic Discipline: Fast forward to 1956, a pivotal year when the term "Artificial Intelligence" was coined by John McCarthy at the Dartmouth Conference. This gathering of brilliant minds is widely acknowledged as the official starting point of AI as a field of study. The conference set out to explore the hypothesis that "every aspect of learning or any other feature of intelligence can, in principle, be so precisely described that a machine can be made to simulate it."

The AI Winter: Despite the initial excitement, the road ahead for AI was not smooth. The field experienced what is known as the "AI Winter," a period where the promises of AI were met with the harsh reality of technological limitations. Funding dried up, and the interest of the public and private sectors waned. The AI Winter was a time for sober reflection on the grandiose expectations set by the early pioneers.

The Quiet Progress: Yet even as public interest cooled, progress continued. A dedicated group of researchers persisted, working diligently to advance the field. It was during these quieter years that some of the most fundamental aspects of AI as we know it today were developed. The foundations of machine learning, neural networks, and natural language processing were laid during this time, often in academic settings away from the limelight.

The Resurgence and Modern AI: The resurgence of AI came with the advent of the internet and the explosion of data. The availability of large datasets, coupled with advances in computational power, gave AI new life. Machine learning algorithms, fed with data and run on increasingly powerful computers, began to achieve tasks previously thought impossible for machines.

ChatGPT and Generative AI: This historical overview would be incomplete without mentioning ChatGPT, which took the world by storm in November 2022. ChatGPT, developed by OpenAI, is a variant of the GPT (Generative Pretrained Transformer) family, which has been trained on diverse internet text. It can generate human-like text based on the input it receives, making it an advanced example of natural language processing (NLP) in action. This technology is not just about understanding or processing language but also about generating it, opening up new possibilities for human-computer interaction.

The history of AI is woven from many threads of innovation. It begins with Alan Turing and the theoretical underpinnings of computational thought, travels through the ambitious beginnings and sobering winters, and arrives at the modern resurgence fueled by data and computational power. This journey from the past to the present sets the stage for the practical applications reshaping our world.

4.3   The Layers of AI Explained

The realm of Artificial Intelligence is a layered one, much like the concentric circles depicted in the image. It's a hierarchy where each level builds upon the previous, becoming increasingly sophisticated and specialized as we move inward.

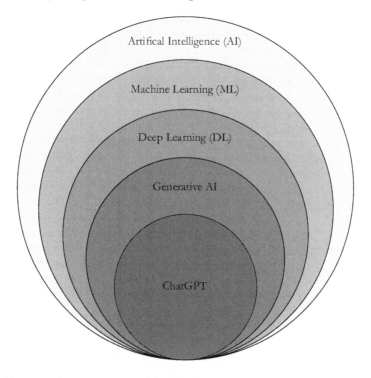

Figure 4: AI encompasses many other disciplines like ML, DL, and Generative AI

Artificial Intelligence (AI) forms the widest circle in the hierarchy of data-driven technology, representing a spectrum of machine-executed tasks requiring human-like intelligence. It's the umbrella term for machines mimicking cognitive functions such as learning and problem-solving.

Within AI sits Machine Learning (ML), where machines improve and learn from data over time without explicit programming. ML is the engine of AI, driving the adaptability and growth of intelligent systems.

Deep Learning (DL) is a specialized subset of ML based on neural networks, designed to recognize patterns and make decisions. DL models, akin to the human brain, interpret complex data through layered architectures, enabling nuanced understanding and prediction.

Generative AI narrows the focus to creation, using learned data patterns to innovate and generate original, realistic outputs, from new images to predictive models.

At the core is ChatGPT, a product of Generative AI by OpenAI. It's an advanced model that generates human-like text, showcasing the pinnacle of current AI's ability to understand and replicate human language.

This tiered model reflects the flow from broad AI applications to the precise capabilities of ChatGPT, demonstrating the layered complexity and refinement of modern AI technology.

4.4   Machine Learning as A Central Part of AI

As we transition from historical context to practical applications, we now turn to Machine Learning (ML), the heartbeat of modern AI. ML is where the abstract theories of the past meet the concrete challenges of the present, offering solutions and driving innovation. It's where we move from asking if machines can think, to teaching them how to learn.

Imagine you're teaching a friend to recognize the difference between cats and dogs. You'd show them pictures of each, pointing out which is which until they get the hang of it. This is a bit like how **Supervised Learning** in AI works.

Computers, much like our friend, learn from examples. We give them lots of labeled pictures – say, "This is a cat" and "This is a dog" – and over time, they learn to tell the difference between the two on their own.

Now, picture a scenario where you give your friend a collection of animal photos without any labels. Some animals might be in unusual poses, others might have distinctive color patterns, and some might be in atypical settings. Without any instructions, your friend starts to group these animals based on their own observations – maybe by the size of the animals, the patterns of their fur, or the environments they're in. This is akin to **Unsupervised Learning** in AI. In this case, the AI is provided with unlabeled data and begins to find patterns and commonalities on its own, organizing the animals into clusters based on the characteristics it autonomously considers relevant.

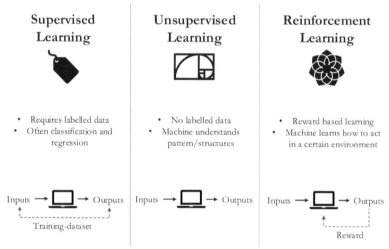

Figure 5: Supervised, Unsupervised, and Reinforcement Learning as three categories of ML

Now, let's say you're teaching your friend to play a video game, and they get points every time they do something right. They'll try different strategies to increase their score, learning the game as they go. This is **Reinforcement Learning**. In AI, we set up a system where the computer tries out different things and gets "rewards" when it does what we want it to do. It's a bit like training a pet with treats.

These different learning strategies come with their own sets of advantages and challenges. Take **Supervised Learning**, for instance. It's like giving direct feedback to your friend about those cat and dog pictures. This feedback loop ensures that the learning is precise, and the model built from this process is usually easier to understand and can be highly accurate, especially when there's plenty of labeled data to learn from. The downside? It requires a hefty amount of this labeled data, which isn't always easy or cheap to come by. Plus, if new data comes along that's too different from the training set, the model might not know what to make of it.

Moving on to **Unsupervised Learning**, imagine your friend sorting those animal photos without any hints. This approach is great for exploring data and finding hidden structures within it since it doesn't need any labels to get started. However, it can be tricky to gauge how effective the model is because the results can be less clear-cut and harder to interpret. It's like trying to understand why your friend grouped those animals together based solely on their own logic.

And then there's **Reinforcement Learning**, akin to guiding your friend through that video game with points as incentives. This method excels in dynamic environments where it can learn from trial and error, adapting its strategy to maximize rewards. It's powerful for complex problems, like teaching robots to navigate or optimizing strategies in games. But it's not without its complexities. It requires a clear reward system to work toward, and it can take a lot of computational power and time to learn effectively, much like a gamer trying to master a new game over many hours of play.

Each of these learning methods has its place in the AI toolkit, and understanding their strengths and limitations is key for decision-makers. Whether it's the direct feedback of Supervised Learning, the pattern discovery of Unsupervised Learning, or the trial-and-error growth of Reinforcement Learning, each contributes to the advancement of AI in unique ways.

4.5   Deep Learning: The Intuition Behind AI

Deep Learning is the next evolution in the AI saga, taking the principles of Machine Learning and applying them in a complex, layered approach akin to the human brain's neural networks. It's about teaching machines to discern not just patterns but also the nuances and contexts of the data they're processing.

To understand Deep Learning, let's extend the analogy of teaching your friend. This time, instead of just recognizing cats and dogs, you're helping them understand the subtleties of animal behavior. It's a more complex task that requires not just identifying the animal but also interpreting its actions and predicting what it might do next.

Deep Learning takes the principles of Machine Learning a step further. It involves layers upon layers of processing units – akin to neurons in the human brain – that work together to understand data in a deep, hierarchical fashion. Think of it as teaching your friend to recognize not just the animal but also to notice the intricate patterns of its fur, the gleam in its eye, and the way it interacts with its environment.

These layers in a Deep Learning model learn to recognize different features of the data. The first layer might pick up on simple patterns, like edges or colors. As you go deeper, subsequent layers combine these simple patterns to recognize more complex features, like shapes, and eventually, whole objects or actions. It's like building a complex understanding from basic building blocks.

One of the most popular types of Deep Learning models is called a Convolutional Neural Network (CNN). These are especially good at handling images. When you show your friend a picture of a cat sitting in a sunny window, a CNN would start by noticing the edges and textures. Further in, another layer might recognize the shape of the cat, and even deeper layers might understand the context of the sunny window and the relaxed posture of the cat basking in the sunlight.

Deep Learning shines when it comes to tasks that require a nuanced understanding of data, like voice recognition, language translation, and image classification. It's the technology behind the face recognition on your smartphone, the voice of your virtual assistant, and even the algorithms that recommend your next favorite show on streaming platforms.

But Deep Learning isn't without its challenges. It requires a significant amount of data to learn effectively and a lot of computational power to process that data. Training a Deep Learning model can be like teaching your friend about animal behavior – it takes time, patience, and a lot of examples. However, once trained, a Deep Learning model can be incredibly powerful, providing insights and automation capabilities that can transform industries.

4.6 Generative AI

Following the exploration of Machine Learning and Deep Learning, we now turn our attention to Generative AI, a remarkable branch of AI that transcends traditional boundaries of data interpretation, venturing into the realms of creation and innovation.

Understanding Generative AI: Generative AI refers to algorithms capable of generating new, original content or data models based on the learning from existing datasets. This form of AI doesn't just analyze or recognize patterns; it creates new content, from realistic images and text to complex simulations.

Capabilities of Generative AI: This AI technology stands at the forefront of creative potential, capable of designing novel concepts and solutions. It can generate realistic visuals, simulate scenarios in various fields, and even create new forms of artistic expression. In essence, it's teaching AI not just to understand the world, but to add to it in meaningful ways.

Applications Across Domains: The applications of Generative AI are vast and varied. It can be employed in diverse fields such as art, where it can create new pieces, in entertainment for generating realistic content, or in research for simulating scientific scenarios. Its ability to generate predictive models also makes it valuable in areas requiring future scenario planning.

The Predictive Edge: Beyond creating tangible outputs, Generative AI can predict outcomes by analyzing existing trends and data. This predictive power can be crucial in fields like climate modeling, financial forecasting, and even medical research, where understanding future trends or outcomes is invaluable.

Navigating the Challenges: With great potential comes significant challenges. Generative AI raises questions about authenticity, ethics in AI-generated content, and the implications of AI-created material in society. Ensuring responsible use and addressing these ethical considerations is crucial for the beneficial application of Generative AI.

The Future of Generative AI: As we continue to refine and develop Generative AI technologies, we're not just enhancing our analytical capabilities; we're endowing AI with a form of creative intelligence. This leap forward opens up new horizons for innovation and creativity, redefining the limits of what AI can achieve.

Generative AI represents a fascinating evolution in the field of artificial intelligence. It's not merely an analytical tool but an engine of creation, offering a glimpse into a future where AI contributes actively to the creative and innovative endeavors of humanity.

For a deeper dive into Generative AI, I'm sharing with you a recording of a talk I gave a few months after ChatGPT became viral:

QR Code 2: Recording of a talk on Generative AI for manufacturing

4.7   The Know-It-All AI Agent

The **AI Agent** represents the culmination of the learning methods discussed earlier, a sophisticated system that integrates supervised, unsupervised, and reinforcement learning, along with the advanced capabilities of deep learning. It's the orchestrator of these tools, the conductor of the AI symphony. Generative AI builds the interface to the human, allowing them to interact naturally with the underlying sophisticated systems.

Imagine a vast library, a compendium of the world's knowledge, with books, digital records, and multimedia spanning the breadth of human thought. In this library, there's an AI Agent, a master orchestrator adept at navigating this sea of information.

This AI Agent is like a supremely knowledgeable librarian who knows every book, article, and film in the library. It doesn't just know where everything is; it understands the content and context of all the information. When you have a question, the AI Agent is your go-to entity, capable of pulling together disparate threads of knowledge to provide comprehensive answers.

The AI Agent employs a variety of methods to serve your information needs. It uses machine learning to recognize patterns, much like how a librarian might remember which topics are frequently sought after, and guide you to the right section. It queries databases to find the exact book you need at a moment's notice. And it adapts and learns from each interaction, just as a librarian learns from every patron's inquiry to better serve the next.

Deep learning is one of the tools in its arsenal, allowing the AI Agent to delve into complex queries and provide nuanced insights. It's not limited to predefined rules; it can learn from data in ways that mimic human intuition, yet on a scale and speed that far surpasses our own capabilities.

The AI Agent is not just a passive repository of information. It actively manages knowledge, ensuring that the library's contents are always current, relevant, and accessible. It oversees the ingestion of new data, categorizing and indexing each piece for easy retrieval. This process is meticulous and continuous, reflecting the ever-evolving landscape of information.

In this digital library, the AI Agent facilitates an iterative problem-solving process. It's a dynamic conversation, where each query is a prompt for the AI to refine its search and understanding, ensuring that the results are tailored to the specific needs of the inquiry.

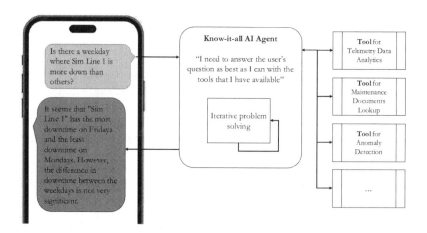

Figure 6: The Know-it-all AI agent

The AI Agent is a universal solution, transcending the boundaries of any single field or industry. It's as valuable to a manufacturing manager seeking to optimize a production line as it is to a researcher exploring the frontiers of science. It represents a leap forward in how we interact with and leverage the vast amounts of data at our disposal.

In essence, the AI Agent is the embodiment of our collective intelligence, amplified by the power of artificial intelligence. It's the ultimate partner in the quest for knowledge, providing a bridge between the questions we have and the answers that lie within the expanse of human knowledge.

4.8   Key Takeaways

As we distill the essence of this chapter, it is essential to focus on the foundational terms that underpin the field of Artificial Intelligence:

Artificial Intelligence (AI): This is the overarching domain within computer science dedicated to crafting systems capable of tasks that would typically necessitate human intellect. It's the umbrella under which various forms of computational intelligence reside.

Machine Learning (ML): A pivotal subset of AI, Machine Learning is the engine that powers AI's ability to learn from experience. It's the method through which machines can improve their performance on tasks over time. ML is primarily divided into three categories:

- **Supervised Learning**: This method involves learning from a dataset that has been labeled in advance. It's akin to learning with a guide, where the outcomes are known, and the task is to predict future results based on this labeled data.
- **Unsupervised Learning**: Here, the learning occurs without pre-labeled answers. The system is tasked with identifying patterns and structures within the

data on its own, much like finding order in chaos without a predefined roadmap.

- **Reinforcement Learning**: This type of learning is about making decisions and learning from the consequences. It's a trial-and-error approach where actions are taken, and rewards or penalties are given based on the correctness of the action.

Generative AI: A cutting-edge branch of AI that goes beyond data analysis to generate new, original content or data models. It has the potential for creative and predictive applications, raising new possibilities and ethical considerations in AI's role.

AI Agent: An AI Agent stands as a culmination of ML techniques, a sophisticated entity that can employ supervised, unsupervised, and reinforcement learning to perform complex tasks. It's an orchestrator of these tools, capable of navigating vast data terrains, making decisions, and learning from interactions. An AI Agent can be thought of as the conductor of an orchestra, ensuring that each section plays in harmony to achieve a collective goal.

These terms are not just jargon; they are the keystones for understanding AI's capabilities and limitations. They serve as a common language for discussing the transformative impact of AI across various sectors. As we progress further into the realm of AI, these concepts will serve as guideposts, helping us to navigate the more intricate implications of Artificial Intelligence.

5

AI: FUELING THE FLYWHEEL

In this critical chapter, I weave together the transformative power of Artificial Intelligence (AI) with the dynamic Flywheel concept, illustrating how AI not only complements but significantly propels each step of the Industry 4.0 journey. Here, I offer insights on leveraging AI within each of the four flywheel steps: Collecting Data, Communicating Data, Predicting and Detecting, and Recommending and Acting.

The Industry 4.0 Flywheel represents a cycle of continuous improvement and momentum. When AI is integrated into this model, it supercharges each phase, infusing the cycle with advanced capabilities and insights. Think about the role of AI as an enabler that makes the flywheel easier to turn.

Through diving into the 4 steps, I will build out a generalized, high-level "architecture." While there are many possible ways to implement it in detail, the majority of modern implementations that I came across follow this pattern in its essence.

There are many nuances to it, and the intent is not to outline a reference software architecture but to illustrate the basic data flows to get from raw data to actions.

Furthermore, I will steer clear from choosing or highlighting specific technological choices. This, similar to the use cases, is highly dependent on the circumstances of each company, and there are simply too many variables at play.

Let's start with how we collect data.

5.1 Collecting Data with AI

In the digital fabric of Industry 4.0, data runs through the veins of every process, vital to its very existence. The quest for data collection may seem herculean, particularly within corporate structures, but the approach does not need to be exhaustive from the outset.

Consider data as the initial thrust needed to set the Industry 4.0 Flywheel in motion – integral, yes, but overwhelming, not necessarily. The key is *not* to attempt to get data from every possible source immediately. Begin modestly; target the low-hanging fruits. Whether it's a piece of machinery or just a single sensor, starting small enables you to construct a lightweight, manageable flywheel.

A useful analogy here is the Minimum Viable Product (MVP) definition often used in the startup or Agile context. An MVP is the smallest possible scope in the development of a product that still provides value. The idea is to develop an MVP, get it into the market, and receive feedback. Then iterate over and over again. MVP is basically the first turn of the smallest flywheel that makes sense to build. From there on, the start of every iteration spins the flywheel.

The immediate action here is to find your version of the MVP of data source(s) within your company. It should be as small in scope as possible while still making it useful.

A single sensor measuring the quality of parts in an interim process might be such an example. It might be as little as collecting a single signal (also called a tag) from this sensor that measures the diameter of a hole. If there is a change in the diameter, you can infer that the driller needs to be replaced. Furthermore, you can use it to make an interim continuous quality check. If the diameter is outside of the specification, the part gets removed from the line.

Having a single measurement as your MVP might be an edge scenario and work only in some cases. For others, it might need to be as large as a small production line. While this is certainly larger in scope, it might still be manageable, especially when the line is controlled by a single unit that is easy to get access to.

From Bronze to Gold

There are multiple paradigms on how to structure a data pipeline. I chose to outline the Bronze-to-Gold pattern in this book as it allows me to illustrate the evolution of data through the stages of collection, cleaning, and contextualization (also referred to as Medallion Architecture).

The central idea of Bronze-to-Gold is that data is incrementally refined, cleaned, and augmented with context.

It has multiple transformations, turning raw information into strategic gold.

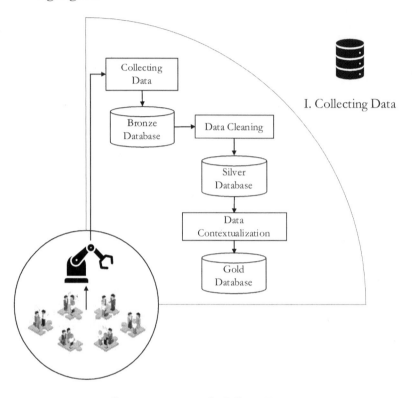

Figure 7: zoom-in on the Collecting Data step

Data Sources: It all starts with data sources. Here, the raw data is generated from a variety of origins, including sensors, logs, and other information systems within the manufacturing environment. Each source emits a stream of data, which needs to be captured and analyzed to extract value.

Data Collector: Serving as the interim layer, the data collector is responsible for gathering information from multiple sources. The Data Collector is able to speak the language of the data source and convert that into a single common language and structure suitable for feeding into the Bronze Database.

Bronze Database: This initial repository is where the unprocessed data resides. Think of it as a preliminary archive that holds the raw material. In the Bronze Database, the data might be voluminous and unstructured, but it represents the potential that can be unlocked through further processing.

Data Cleaning: Before it can be utilized effectively, the data needs to be cleaned. This process involves filtering out noise, correcting errors, and normalizing the data to ensure consistency. Data cleaning is critical as it ensures the quality and reliability of the data before it progresses to the next stage.

Silver Database: Once cleaned, the data is transferred to the Silver Database. This stage is crucial for preparing the data for more sophisticated analytics that drive strategic decisions.

Data Contextualization: The transformation from Silver to Gold involves adding context to the data. This means enriching the data with additional metadata, categorizing it, and linking it to other relevant data points to provide a multi-dimensional view. It's this depth of insight that turns the cleaned data into actionable intelligence.

Gold Database: The final destination in this journey is the Gold Database. It's the vault where the most refined and valuable data is stored. At this stage, the data is not only clean and organized but also enriched with context, making it ready for deeper levels of analysis and decision-making.

Note, that this is a generic theme and concept, but your reality might look different. E.g., you might end up with interim databases between Bronze-Silver-Gold to segment the transformation process further – or have multiple Gold databases to leverage the pros and cons of different database types. While these details are of great importance, they go beyond the scope of this book.

How AI Can Help

In the context of the journey from data collection to the Gold Database, Artificial Intelligence (AI) enhances each step of the process:

In Data Collection: AI can be utilized to optimize the data collection process. Intelligent algorithms can determine the most relevant data to collect, reducing noise and focusing on information that offers the most significant potential for insights. It has the potential to remove the manual work of selecting labels.

During Data Cleaning: AI excels in identifying and correcting errors in large datasets. Machine learning models can be trained to detect data quality issues, fill in missing values, and ensure consistency across different data sources.

For Data Contextualization: AI can automate the categorization of data and enhance it with relevant metadata. Natural Language Processing (NLP) can extract meaning from text data, and pattern recognition can link related data points, adding a layer of context that transforms clean data into actionable insights.

Scaling to the Gold Database: As the volume of data increases, AI can scale the data cleaning and contextualization processes efficiently. It can handle the increasing complexity without a proportional increase in resources, maintaining high data quality standards.

Continuous Improvement: AI is not static; it learns and improves over time. As more data flows through the process, AI algorithms adapt, improving their accuracy in data cleaning and contextualization, which results in a continuously refined Gold Database.

By harnessing the power of AI, the data transformation journey becomes not just more efficient but also more dynamic. AI's capability to learn and adapt ensures that the data not only meets current needs but also evolves to anticipate future challenges, ensuring that the manufacturing processes stay ahead in the Industry 4.0 revolution.

Key Considerations

When initiating the first step of the Industry 4.0 Flywheel – Collecting Data with AI – critical challenges and considerations must be addressed to ensure a seamless and scalable foundation for future growth:

Old Machines: A common argument is that older machinery does not offer enough data points to be of use. My experience is different. Even if there are not hundreds of measurements, there is still something to be extracted. And there is always the option to add additional sensors to collect further data points. When making a purchasing decision, keep in mind that the machine is ready for data collection.

Some original equipment manufacturers, "OEMs," are significantly more advanced than others.

Network Infrastructure: Establishing a robust network connection between the plant floor and data management systems, whether on-premises or cloud-based, is crucial. This involves:

- Ensuring reliable connectivity between data sources and the data collector. Often referred to as the Operational Technology (OT) level.
- Securing the data transfer from the data collector to the Bronze database, whether that database resides on-prem or in the cloud. This is usually part of the Information Technology (IT) domain.

In most scenarios, the Data Collector will be an on-prem deployment that sits close to the plant floor. It is sometimes also referred to as an IoT/IIoT gateway.

Scalability: The system must be designed to handle an increasing number of data tags and sources without performance degradation. The architecture, especially the databases and the data pipeline from Bronze to Gold, must support scalability. Avoiding scalability issues is essential for maintaining the momentum of the flywheel, ensuring that the increasing volume and complexity of data do not hinder its acceleration.

Scalability is one of the key advantages of deploying the solution to the Cloud. It merely takes the click of a button to add more storage and compute resources (compared to buying new servers). For on-prem deployments, advanced technologies like Kubernetes clusters[a] are necessary to enable high scale. This is both expensive to set up but also to run and maintain. However, it could be a preferred option if you have an excellent IT team.

The best and most flexible (but not easiest) approach is to build the solution cloud and on-prem agnostic, such that you can deploy it on any Cloud, on-prem, and anything hybrid. Be mindful when choosing vendors. Double-check that their solution is built flexible enough to allow switching Cloud providers and on-prem deployments.

Privacy and Security: Ensuring your data is kept private and secure is absolutely key. I'll only quickly touch on this topic as there are countless other books out there that specifically focus on this topic. Also note that 100% secure does not exist; there is *always* some remaining risk.

It's similar to the security of a house. Most people would say their house is secure, but it is never 100% secure. What they are really saying it is *secure enough*. The front door might have one or two locks, but why not have three or four or even more? Intuitively, you understand there is a diminishing return with every lock added.

---

[a] Kubernetes acts as a smart conductor for the software world, orchestrating a fleet of containers – each a self-contained environment with its program – across a group of machines called a cluster. It ensures these containers run harmoniously, balancing their workload, and stepping in to heal the system automatically if something goes wrong, much like a maestro ensuring the music plays on, even if a violin string snaps.

The same is true for privacy and security when it comes to data. Unfortunately, the complexity is significantly higher, and it's harder to develop an intuition for what *secure enough* means.

I found that one of the best questions to ask is: "What happens if somebody can break into my system, mess with it, and data is leaked?" The following discussions are then focused on the consequences and sensitivity of the data.

As an example, if, on one side, the data in question is bank details and social security numbers of your employees, then an incident might mean the end of your company. So *secure enough* usually means very secure (that's why the gold reserves from central banks are behind layers of vaults and security).

On the other side, let's say the data is temperature measurements *without* metadata, context, company, or machine info. Of course, you never want this data to become public, but the impact will likely be (very) minor. The data in the Bronze database is such an example.

Now, I'm certainly not implying to act recklessly and not prioritize privacy and security, but I do want to highlight focusing on *secure enough*.

It's also important to note that the further down the data pipeline data flows, the higher the value becomes. Leaks from the Gold database are already more critical as data is contextualized.

Data Retention and Backups: It seems obvious to ensure data is backed up. However, since data volumes are high, the right systems need to be in place to create these backups. If a repeatable processing approach exists to convert data from Bronze to Gold, it might be enough to focus the backup on the Bronze database. In case of data loss, data can be replayed from the Bronze.

Deciding on the retention period is also critical. Retention is how long the data is kept in the database before it is deemed too old and is deleted. To start with, I would aim for an unlimited retention period. And then, over time, refine it.

Also note that strategies exist that allow moving data from "hot" storage into "cold," which basically means a (significantly) reduced cost at the expense of a longer retrieval time.

Iterative Tagging Approach: Begin with a manageable number of tags to implement an end-to-end data collection process. Think MVP. This helps to identify any initial bottlenecks or challenges without being overwhelmed by volume. For the initial tags, prioritize them based on their potential impact and relevance to key operational insights.

It is important to avoid having the tag selection step be a blocker to test the Data Collection pipeline. Start with a handful of tags – relevant or not – to establish the initial data flow and test the pipeline.

Then, you can incrementally add more tags, refining the process with each addition. This iterative approach unblocks subsequent steps, allowing the flywheel to start turning and generating value.

The More Tags, the Better: This is a controversial topic, but my clear opinion is that the more tags you have, the better. Especially in early phases, don't try to be over-selective which tags you push down the pipeline. There are two main reasons for this:

1. You simply don't know which tags will become important in the future. It's a learning phase, and you cannot recover data that you never collected. The opportunity cost is too high.
2. It's very cheap. More tags do not cost you significantly more if you have a scalable infrastructure in place.

That being said, the cost of processing becomes higher the further down the pipeline you go, and especially once we look into the subsequence step of the flywheel. Hence, you might choose to collect everything you can and dump it into the Bronze store. Then, filter what you process further to Silver and Gold.

Sampling Frequency: Analog sensors like temperature are constantly measuring values. When collecting data, we need to be specific about the frequency we want these data points to be captured. I have seen ranges from hundreds of milliseconds to a couple of minutes.

My arguments here are similar to the "The more tags, the better" consideration. If you have a modern, scalable pipeline, having data from hundreds of thousands of sensors every second shouldn't be a problem.

Especially in the beginning, I recommend starting with 1 second. Whether you aggregate the 1-second data when moving from Bronze to Gold is another topic.

Once you understand how you leverage the data, you *might* think about reducing the frequency to reduce unnecessary volume. But again, cost of storage and processing is usually low compared to potential opportunity cost of missing critical interim data points.

Besides frequency, you will also often hear *on change* which means that data is only transmitted when the value changes. That is a very useful method for *some* tags, especially metadata, but generally adds significant complexity to the processing layers as interim data points need to be inferred and interpolated. With the risk of repeating myself too often, it falls into the "optimize later" category for me.

Keep things simple, think about MVP, and if data volume becomes an issue already in the early days, you need to rethink the data pipeline and work on a scalable architecture. Reducing the data volume is only an interim treatment of symptoms, and it will come back to bite you eventually.

From now onward, we consider the Gold Database to serve as a single source of truth for the subsequent steps of visualization, predictions, and actionable insights.

5.2 Communicating Data with AI

When we've gathered and refined data into a Gold Database, visualizing this data becomes our next step. It's all about making data accessible and starting to unlock its potential for the entire team.

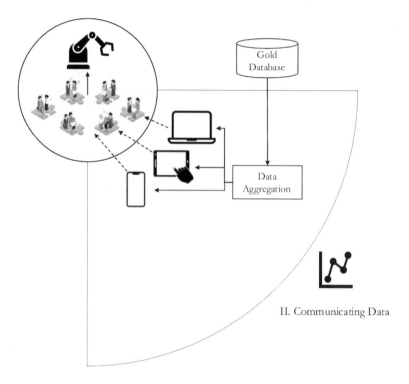

Figure 8: zoom-in into the Communicating Data step

Business Intelligence (BI) Tools and Their Limitations

Dashboards are commonly used for data visualization. While many Business Intelligence (BI) tools are available, they tend to struggle with the large data volumes typical in Industry 4.0. While the gold database contains curated data, there is often an aggregation and analytics layer required to crunch that data into something meaningful to display in real time[b].

As an example, let's say you have 100 pumps across your production facility with data being collected every 1 second. If you are interested in which pump had the highest temperature over the last month, there are ~260 million data points that need to be considered[c]. To find the answer to the question, you need to find the maximum value and then the associated pump (the ArgMax function for people familiar).

Without going into further detail, you can see from the image that this needs some advanced technology to be able to query big data within a time that is acceptable for a user to wait (< 1-3 seconds).

The good news is that these technologies are available, and querying that set of data is no longer a big challenge. The technology is there to handle trillions and quadrillion of data points without an issue.

Unfortunately, I still hear a lot of issues around "the data volume is too big, and we need to focus on the important tags, otherwise the visualization freezes."

While inherently there is nothing wrong with focusing on the important tags, it is not solving the problem. As it is treating

---

[b] Pre-compute and caching techniques, of course, exist and have their time and place. However, it's impossible to pre-compute everything the user might be interested in. See following arguments about the know-it-all AI agent.

[c] $100 \; pumps \cdot 3600 \frac{s}{h} \cdot 24 \frac{h}{day} \cdot 30 \; days = 259{,}200{,}000 \; datapoints$

the symptoms instead of looking at the root cause – which turns out to be incorrect or outdated technology in 99% of the cases.

If the above sounds familiar, I encourage you to focus on eliminating the root cause. And this goes for in-house-built solutions as well as solutions from vendors. The cost of switching to a scalable technology becomes significantly higher the further down the road you are. And worst, you risk that the flywheel will eventually come to a grinding hold.

Consider the following case study:

At MontBlancAI, we worked with an OEM that had an internally grown solution consisting of basically a SQL database structure to store their telemetry data and PowerBI dashboards for visualization. The first couple of weeks things looked great, and the company was able to turn the Flywheel. Data was visualized, predictions were made, and actions were taken. However, after three months, nothing worked anymore, and the data volume became too large for the database and dashboard to handle. Things slowed down, the flywheel came to a stop, and so did the project.

During the first conversations with them, their primary concern was about data volume and the need to be very selective about tags. We did challenge them with the promise that our solution (= modern and well-chosen technology) is highly scalable, and the number of tags would not affect performance. And even after months and years, things are as fast as they were in the beginning.

While I mentioned scalability as a key consideration already during the first step of Data Collection, it often doesn't show until the visualization layer is added. At this step, the database is queried, and aggregation and analytics need to be performed in real time to display what the users are interested in.

And, as we saw, many traditional databases and BI tools are not designed to provide that kind of scale on top of trillions and quadrillions of records.

Data Democratization.

Industry 4.0 is a great chance to empower workers. Data should be accessible to everyone in the organization – of course, within reasonable limits. When in doubt, and especially in the beginning stages, I recommend leaning toward oversharing instead of over-constraining. Making data widely available fosters a culture of engagement and insight-driven decision-making.

One of the most powerful impacts of AI within the flywheel is that it makes powerful technology *accessible to everyone*. And it starts with creating the right visualization for the right people. And it does go beyond static dashboards. It's more interactive and allows everyone to leverage data without the need for a data science degree.

AI's Role in Visualization

Dashboards have been around for a long time and are useful lenses for data. However, they have clear limitations. Creating dashboards for every need is simply impractical.

And that's where AI can be incredibly useful. Allowing users to interact with data and create customized insights, perhaps through an AI-assisted chat function or automated reports.

You can – with reasonable effort – build an AI that summarizes your production data and sends personalized daily or weekly reports to your team. With feedback, it will improve over time to make the reports more useful to the individual needs. The plant manager will only get the most significant changes, while the machine operator on the plant floor will see every bit about their machine.

This drives data democratization as it makes data more user-friendly and widely accessible, similar to how tools like ChatGPT have brought advanced AI models to a broad audience.

There is immense complexity behind the scenes, but none of that is visible to the users. Whenever I come across legacy tools, it seems to me the complete opposite. To be able to navigate their user interface you need weeks of training, while the functionality of the tool doesn't warrant that complexity. The main reason for this is that it takes less effort to make something simple look complex compared to making something complex look easy. AI allows you to achieve the latter.

Considerations for Effective Data Visualization

Beyond Traditional Dashboards: I discussed dashboards and the limitations of BI tools above. While I focused on the scalability aspect, I want to highlight here another point. What you are using for data visualization will evolve rapidly into a more interactive platform with predictions and insights in the subsequent steps of the flywheel. It will become significantly more specialized and customized to your Industry 4.0 scenarios. Furthermore, it becomes the cockpit for your AI.

As you don't want to end up with a handful or more disconnected user interfaces, it's important to make the right choices about the visualization platform. The choice is less important for the first few turns of the flywheel but becomes very important later on. When building in-house, it's okay to start with BI tools that allow you to quickly iterate. However, once you see that too many workarounds have to be implemented, consider investing in a dedicated platform (or bringing a vendor on board).

Vendor Capabilities: Whether you build your Industry 4.0 tooling completely in-house or buy off the shelf, you will interface with vendors to some degree. It might just be the database or aggregation layer. In either case, ensure that the vendor allows your solution to scale, be responsive, and be easy and fun to use.

Availability on Multiple Devices: Whether you are sitting at a desk or walking around the factory floor, the information you need should always be accessible. With the right technologies, it's easier than ever to bring it across mobile and desktop devices. Leverage the strength of each device type. Deep dive data investigations are most likely happening on the desktop. Push notifications about alarms are ideal for mobile apps on everyone's phone. A huge TV is ideal for displaying productivity statistics from the line and providing real-time feedback on how the production is running.

Beautiful Design, Easy and Fun to Use: Most consumer applications have thoughtful design. It's enjoyable to use them (for the most part, at least). Compare that to most of the applications found in the business context. In many cases, it's simply frustrating and requires hours and hours of training.

Easy-to-use design will not only reduce your training costs but also drive adoption across teams and departments. Additionally, you will be forced in the process to focus on the core. As I mentioned before, developing complex systems to look simple is hard – but it pays off.

To sum it up: visualizing data in Industry 4.0 is about turning complex data into an accessible and interactive resource. It's a key step in turning data into insights and actions, helping to inform decisions and strategies across the organization. When reaching this step, it opens up the opportunity to generate tremendous amounts of value. AI is there to help abstract complexity and make insights accessible to everyone.

5.3   Predicting and Detecting with AI

As we delve deeper into the capabilities of AI and ML in the context of Industry 4.0, we enter the realm of predicting outcomes and detecting anomalies. This is where the true potential of AI starts to shine – unsupervised, and supervised ML.

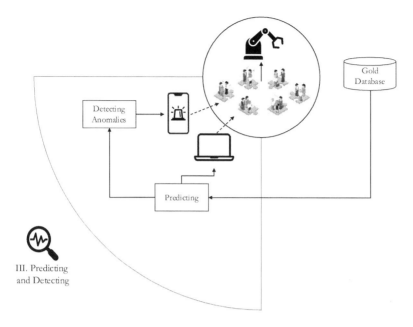

Figure 9: zoom-in into the Predicting and Detecting step

The Continuous Process of ML

At the core is ML as a process that operates tirelessly in the background, analyzing and interpreting data from the Gold Database. This process is all about making predictions about future outcomes and detecting anomalies. ML is continuously crunching data and transforming it in a variety of ways.

Typically, it is not a single ML model running, but an army focusing on different aspects. It follows the paradigm of dividing and conquering (which seems to be a universal truth, as I remember my professor saying this in just about every project meeting).

For example, there might be an ML model specifically trained to predict the OEE of a line for the upcoming day. Or a model automatically learning the standard temperature curve of a tank when it is being cleaned.

The Power of Predictions

To grasp the power of these predictions, consider this analogy:

If I'd tell you the stock value of gold from yesterday, how useful would that be for you? Well, not much, I presume. You can simply look it up on your favorite trading website.

But what about if I can predict it five minutes from now? This is probably more valuable, as it offers some last-minute trading opportunities.

And what about being able to predict it one month from now with high accuracy? You might just go off and sell everything you have and make the bet on gold. Presuming my prediction was correct, you will never have to work again and, most likely, also stop reading this book. That's the value of predictions – they become more valuable the higher the accuracy is and further ahead they can predict.

Now, think through what valuable predictions might look like for your factory.

Knowing that a pump is failing in three weeks gives you a window to schedule maintenance and avoid downtime.

Being able to predict the throughput of your production line for the upcoming months more accurately allows you to commit to more products for your customers.

Detecting quality issues early in the process allows you to adjust the process before a concerning product arrives at your customer's warehouse.

Being able to predict the influence of outside humidity on your product quality allows you to implement countermeasures.

Many of these scenarios tie in closely with the mechanics of how anomalies are detected in ML systems.

Detecting Anomalies

Identifying outliers rely on predictions made by ML models. The act of detecting an anomaly is then simply comparing the new, current, and incoming data with the predictions. The difference defines the severity of the anomaly. Typically, there is a threshold under which the deviation is considered to be "normal."

If the model predicts a "normal" range of 20-30 degrees Celsius/Fahrenheit for a temperature sensor and the new measurement is 31, it might not be too bad. Severity is low. But if the value is 60, something is off by quite a bit.

It reminds me of the time I owned an old Volkswagen T4 minivan. I loved the car and still become nostalgic when thinking about it, but that's beside the point.

The car had high mileage and made all types of sounds. Whenever I picked up somebody who hadn't been in my car before, the concerning question inevitably came up: "Sounds like something is broken; is that normal?" As always, I answered, "Yes, it's always like that. You will get used to it."

When we say "getting used to," what we really mean is that our brain starts to *learn* something as being normal – in that case – the sound profile of my car.

However, when there is a deviation strong enough, we detect it as an anomaly, which happened when the rear mount of the exhaust of my T4 minivan broke, and the exhaust was scratching on the asphalt while driving on the highway (true story!). To my surprise, it was not as noisy as you would have thought it might be, but the sound profile was just off. Me and my friend looked at each other and immediately said, "There is something off. Let's stop at the next parking lot and have a look." We couldn't put our finger on it, but we knew that was not what normal sounded like.

Our brain continuously compared the learned sound profile of what was normal with the actual sounds (the incoming data stream). We noticed a deviation strong enough (= an anomaly) to look at each other's faces and act.

ML is doing the same. As an industry example, let's take the vibration of a pump.

The ML model learns the signature of how the pump vibrates under normal conditions. It then compares the incoming vibration data with what the models consider to be normal. The nature and degree of deviation is then an indication of an anomaly, and it can further predict when maintenance is required and understand cause and effect.[d]

Imagine driving a car without our brain being able to learn the sound profile (or vibration profile, for that matter). We wouldn't have been able to detect the scratching exhaust and would have continued driving until something seriously broke that stopped the car. That would likely have resulted in a heavy repair bill, plus some unplanned downtime.

But isn't that exactly what's happening in the majority of machinery and factories today? Equipment is operated until it fails, then teams rush to find replacement parts on-site and the right person who knows how to repair it. If unsuccessful, you have to call your OEM's service team to rush deliver the part the next day (if you are in luck), costing you a fortune plus some even more costly unplanned downtime.

Wouldn't it be better to know these things in advance? To be able to predict and detect? That's exactly where ML comes in. ML is able to predict and detect *at scale* and *automatically*. An army of ML models is relentlessly being trained on quadrillions of data points of your production data. Each of the tens and hundreds of thousands of new and incoming

---

[d] Predicting maintenance of pumps is just one use case of AI. It can also be used to monitor cavitation related issues by contextualizing the pump's data with tank levels from upstream and downstream systems. Or AI can optimize overall system power consumption through shifting the operating points of pumps into their most efficient spot.

data points is being compared to these models per second. Deviations are scored, and anomalies are detected.

From Predictions and Anomalies to People

Once ML is doing its job and an anomaly is detected, alarms and notifications can be triggered. Depending on the severity, the appropriate personnel within the organization is notified.

These predictions and anomalies need to be communicated effectively. This is where an advanced user interface (UI) comes into play, going beyond simple dashboards. It's more interactive, more live, and more reactive.

It switches the primary use of the system from passive (= the user actively looks at the system and investigates an issue) to active (= the system reaches out to the user on issues). A dashboard is passive by its very definition. That switch from passive to active also requires additional interfaces to the user through email, escalation systems, text, calls, push notifications, or others.

Unsupervised Learning and its Pitfalls

Remember the unsupervised learning technique from earlier where the ML automatically found a pattern in a set of pictures that showed animals? That's the core to implementing ML *at scale*. The more you can create an unsupervised prediction system to start with, the better, otherwise, you risk grinding to a hold by overwhelming your team with labeling work (= telling the system which picture is a cat and which is a dog).

Yes, unsupervised learning is harder and less "accurate" to start with. However, with the right strategy, it opens up the right path. Let's understand a bit more about how ML systems can be inaccurate. And, spoiler alert, they all are to some degree, no matter what vendors might tell you.

The first one is *false positives*, and basically all ML systems suffer from this. ML detects something and gives it a high severity, but it turns out to be nothing in the end. Think about it as an emergency call from your doctor. You rush to the hospital, but it turns out you are all healthy. You will lose trust in your doctor very quickly if this repeats a few times too often.

The second one is *false negatives*. The ML doesn't raise an alarm, but there is indeed something going wrong – like a pump breaking down. Your doctor doesn't call you, but it turns out that you have a condition. These are tricky cases because if you never find out that something was wrong and it turns out not to be severe, trust in your doctor remains unchanged. Yet, if indeed something severe is wrong and you notice it, you will immediately lose trust because the doctor missed something.

While ML is a great technology, it's not perfect. It needs to learn over time, so there is generally a trade-off between the number of *false positives* and *false negatives*. For medical issues, we might tolerate a reasonable rate of *false positives* to avoid actually missing a real issue.

However, in the early days of Industry 4.0, I'm arguing that it should be the opposite. The system should keep the number of *false positives* manageable with the risk of increasing the rate of *false negatives* (= missed issues). And my arguments are the following:

A few is better than none. The baseline situation is that most issues remain undetected until they cause a breakdown. So, any incremental improvement is better. Detecting a few *true positives* (these are the ones where your doctor calls you and there is indeed something wrong) is already offering great value. Detecting most pump failures ahead of time is better than letting all of them break down.

There is a diminishing return. There will be diminishing returns when we allow all alarms – even the less severe ones – to propagate. We might identify 10% more of the pump failures ahead of time, but at what cost? Most likely by having to investigate 2-3 times more alarms.

It will make AI look like a joke. Too many *false positives* will kill motivation and trust. After the first couple of alarms that are *not* an issue, people will think that this is all not working. Adoption will be tough, and recovering from that perception is lengthy. Getting the first few alarms right is absolutely critical.

User Feedback

Once you've found the right balance and alarms are being investigated and actions taken, ensure that feedback collection is natural. Don't create a form that takes forever to fill out. Generative AI is a great technology here to create personalized conversations and automatically classify them. That feedback is then fed back into the anomaly detection pipeline, and the labeling starts. The ML becomes smarter over time.

The more natural and organic the labeling process appears, the faster the system learns and the better it will become in terms of false positives and false negatives.

Other ML Use-Cases

The reader with deeper ML experience might argue that there are many other ways to leverage ML for Industry 4.0. And yes, they are absolutely right; there is an endless number of opportunities. I intentionally avoided creating an exhaustive list that would end up being incomplete. And as you might suspect, the list depends on the specifics of each company.

The focus of this book is not to be a reference textbook but to be informative and inspiring to the general reader. Hence, the focus is on predicting and detecting since this is the most common and intuitive use of ML that I've come across. I've seen it across industries and companies, and I consider it a fundamental principle.

Outlining the mechanics of ML behind predicting and detecting gives the reader a starting point to develop their own use cases of ML and have the understanding and vocabulary to communicate effectively with vendors.

Key Takeaways

The key takeaways of this section are:

1. **Predicting:** automatically train models with unsupervised ML, hence, removing labeling work and allowing scale.

2. **Detecting:** favor a limited number of *false positives* to manage the number of alarms your team has to work through. Ensure the first couple of alarms are spot on to earn trust.

3. **Feedback**: create a natural and organic way for users to provide feedback (= labeling). See if you can find ways to make it fun, a game, or even a competition.

4. **Continuous Improvement:** ensure the hard-earned feedback is used within the ML learning process. You should see a reduction in the number of *false positives* and be able to uncover *false negatives* that you missed before. You know you are on the right track if you hear conversations along the lines of, "Oh, weird, we are getting alarms about issues now that we didn't receive before."

Predicting outcomes with AI in Industry 4.0 is about leveraging the power of ML to foresee future scenarios, detect anomalies, and enhance decision-making processes. This approach not only adds significant value to the manufacturing process but also drives continuous improvement as the system learns and adapts over time together with your team.

5.4 Recommending and Acting with AI

The final stage in leveraging AI within the Industry 4.0 framework is about recommending and acting. This stage marks the point where the predictions and anomalies generated by ML are translated into tangible, real-world outcomes.

Too often, Industry 4.0 initiatives don't focus enough on this critical step. They stop when data is collected and visualized and, at best, when predictions and detections are made. In successful cases, actions are derived from these earlier stages, and change is enacted.

However, that leaves step four untouched, which is a very strong, intentional focus on extracting recommendations and actions from data. It closes the control loop.

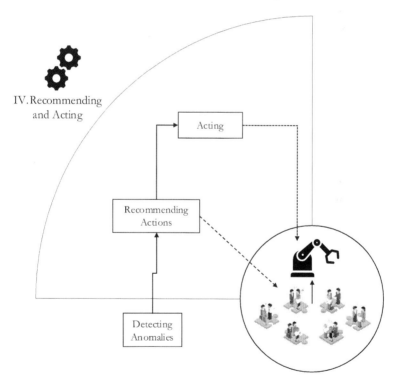

Figure 10: zoom-in into the Recommending and Acting step

Human-Centric Initial Phase

The steps so far can (and should) be highly automated. Data is collected, transformed, and stored automatically. ML models are trained to predict and detect.

You might recall the discussion about the inaccuracy of ML and that ML (and, by extension, AI) is not perfect. Therefore, letting AI act autonomously is not something I would recommend at all – except for maybe some specific cases. My view might, and hopefully will, change once further advancements are made.

Besides the imperfection of AI, there are also considerable technological and organizational challenges.

So far, data has been flowing one way from the machinery to the ML and AI systems. For an autonomous AI, another path needs to be created, letting control data flow from the AI to the machinery. From a purely technical perspective, that is a challenge but also severely increases the impact of security and privacy breaches.

Remember the guiding question I gave about security and privacy? "What happens if somebody can break into my system and data is leaked?"

When creating a channel for AI to control machinery, then a successful cyberattack has the potential to not only stop your complete production but could have even more destructive consequences.

For these reasons, I see the primary role of AI as recommending actions that are then executed by humans. It's crucial to keep humans in the loop, allowing them to make the final decision based on AI's suggestions. AI will not replace humans anytime soon.

Evolving Toward Autonomous AI

Over time, and as the technology matures, AI might evolve to a more advanced stage where it can autonomously execute actions, thereby closing the control loop with machinery.

We are basically creating a Programmable Logic Controller "PLC" control loop on an IT level based on ML and AI. If you run into such a scenario, I highly recommend double-checking if you cannot push that control loop onto the PLC and OT layer and remove the non-deterministic ML and AI components. In many cases, that is possible and will result in a much more robust and secure solution.

Impact through Action

It's important to recognize that measurable improvements in processes and operations are only realized when actions are taken. Everything prior to this stage – data collection, visualization, and prediction – sets the stage for these impactful actions.

As one of the most famous sayings in manufacturing goes, "If You Can't Measure It, You Can't Improve It," you need to ensure you have the right data collected that indicates what you are trying to achieve so you can make a before and after comparison.

While this is easier said than done, it becomes crucial in Phase 2 when ROI is measured on a monetary basis. Being able to prove that based on an AI recommendation, a change has been implemented that increased the OEE from 45% to 67% will make you and your team look like heroes. And that stage, ROI can be calculated in a straightforward manner.

Ideally, every action results in an improvement and is what drives the monetary ROI. But keep in mind, that even actions that do not result in an improvement provide an ROI. It's just not a monetary ROI but an ROI measured in learning. As another insightful saying goes: "Impactful actions come from experience. And experience comes from acting – successful or not."

Key Considerations

Meaningful Recommendations: AI systems should be designed to deliver meaningful, actionable recommendations to the right people.

Monitoring Human Response: Pay close attention to how personnel responds to and acts on these AI-generated recommendations.

Feedback Loop: Establish a mechanism for feedback, both positive and negative, to be relayed back to the AI system. This feedback is vital for continuous learning and improvement of the AI algorithms.

Cautious Progression to AI Control: Move toward allowing AI to control equipment in small, deliberate steps. This gradual progression helps in ensuring safety and reliability.

Transparency and Trust: Foster a culture of transparency around AI decisions to build trust among the workforce. Understanding why and how AI makes certain recommendations can enhance its acceptance and effective utilization.

Evaluating Impact: Regularly assess the impact of AI-driven actions on efficiency, productivity, and safety. This evaluation can guide further refinements in the AI system.

By carefully navigating these considerations, the integration of AI into action-taking processes within the manufacturing industry can lead to significant advancements in efficiency and innovation. This final stage of the AI flywheel in Industry 4.0 is not just about technology; it's about synergizing human expertise with AI capabilities to drive forward a new era of manufacturing excellence.

5.5   Bringing it all Together

In previous chapters, we explored the pivotal role of AI in energizing the Industry 4.0 Flywheel, dissecting each stage with a focus on data flow and value generation. We have seen how data collection, communication, prediction and detection, and recommendations and action blend into a cohesive narrative of continuous improvement and innovation.

The AI-Propelled Industry 4.0 Flywheel

The diagram (as illustrated in the provided image) encapsulates the AI-augmented process flow within the Industry 4.0 Flywheel. It serves as a visual depiction of the connection between technology and humans, emphasizing the cyclical nature of continuous improvement.

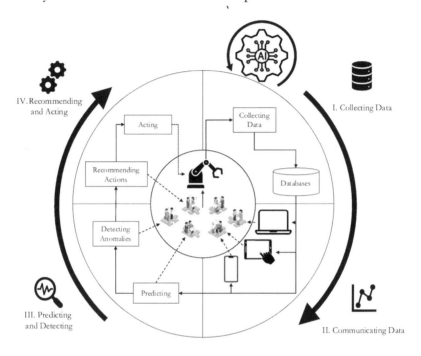

Figure 11: completely zoomed-in Industry 4.0 Flywheel

The diagram is not just a schematic of processes; it is a narrative of progressive human-AI collaboration.

In the second step, humans can interact with data visualization and derive actions to make improvements. This requires significant experience and time.

When moving on to the second and third steps, AI is further processing this data to make it easier for the human to derive actions. Predictions and anomalies pinpoint specific areas of issues or improvements. And when AI is recommending actions, the human just needs to critically review it and execute the action.

With each stage, AI is reducing the cognitive load from the humans' shoulders.

There are five value loops within the flywheel that highlight the evolving role of the human:

1. Data Collection and Communication Loop: Human-Led to AI-Assisted. Initially, users are heavily involved in Data Collecting, selecting sources, and determining metrics. As we step into visualization, the user's burden lightens as AI begins to synthesize and present data in comprehensible formats. The human role here shifts from data handling to data interpretation, transitioning from active participant to insightful observer.

2. Predictive Analysis Loop: Reducing Cognitive Load. In the prediction loop, AI takes on a more prominent role. Users are presented with foresights and trends, relieving them of the need to analyze vast datasets. The cognitive load is significantly reduced as users now focus on understanding AI-generated predictions and preparing strategic responses.

3. Anomaly Detection Loop: Proactive Alerts Minimizing User Involvement. When anomalies arise, the detecting loop alerts users to deviations. This proactive approach means that users no longer need to constantly monitor data streams. Instead, they engage only when necessary, relying on AI to vigilantly oversee operations. The user's role is further simplified to verifying and acting on AI-detected anomalies.

4. Action Recommendation Loop: AI as the Decision Support System. In the recommending action loop, AI elevates its role to an advisor. By suggesting actions, AI alleviates the decision-making load of the user. Here, the user's engagement is more strategic, considering AI's recommendations and deciding on their implementation, marking a shift from decision-maker to decision-approver.

5. Autonomous Action Loop: User as the Overseer. The autonomous action loop represents the pinnacle of the AI journey. The user's role is minimized to an overseer, as AI not only recommends but also implements actions. The loop reflects a near-complete transfer of operational load from user to AI, freeing human intellect for more complex, creative, and strategic tasks.

Evolving User Engagement: From Doers to Directors

As we proceed through the loops, the user's engagement evolves from active doers to strategic directors. The AI Flywheel, depicted in the diagram, illustrates this evolution – a testament to the fact that AI is not replacing human roles but reshaping them. It allows users to ascend from the details of data and processes to innovation and strategy.

By embracing this human-centric AI approach, Industry 4.0 becomes not just a technological revolution but a renaissance of human potential, with AI as the enabler, empowering humans to industrial mastery.

Tomorrow's Factory: Orchestration of the AI-Enhanced Industry Symphony

As we weave the narrative of Tomorrow's Factory with the AI-powered Flywheel, envision a manufacturing landscape transformed by the intelligent orchestration of data and automation.

Imagine stepping onto the factory floor where the air is electric with the hum of machinery, but it's a different kind of energy that underpins this space – the pulsating rhythm of data-driven intelligence. The PLCs, once silent guardians of data, now actively communicate with a central nervous system that spans the entire operation. HMI panels no longer just display data; they interact with it, responding to the touch of human hands that guide them with informed precision.

Sensors that previously fed SCADA servers now contribute to a grand symphony of analytics, their outputs harmonized by AI algorithms into a coherent melody of insights. The "data mess" has been swept away, replaced by a clean, streamlined flow of information that cascades from one process to the next, each step refined by the flywheel's momentum.

The ritual of manual measurements has evolved. Those diligent employees, once isolated in their task of data recording, are now integral players in a system where their insights feed into a loop of continuous improvement. They stand by their stations, tablets in hand, as they oversee the AI's recommendations, tweaking and fine-tuning the machinery like conductors of an industrial orchestra.

The traditional approach, which left you scrambling in response to a customer's distress call, is a tale of the past. Now, when the phone rings, it's not to report a defect but to commend the consistency of your product. The flywheel has spun a new reality into existence – one where a potential issue is anticipated and mitigated, where decisions are made not in days or weeks, but in real-time.

This is the factory where AI does not replace human expertise but amplifies it, where the integration of AI into operations is not a distant dream but a lived experience. Here, innovation is the currency, and those who invest in AI's transformative power are the industry's new leaders.

As the flywheel turns, it generates a current of innovation that propels the factory from the traditional to the transformative. It's in this current that smart factories emerge, differentiated not just by their technology, but by their ability to merge human intuition with AI's predictive prowess.

The time for decision is now — will you cling to the vestiges of the past, or will you ride the wave of the flywheel into the future? The convergence of technology beckons, offering tools and systems that once seemed like the realm of science fiction but are now tangibly within grasp.

6

PEOPLE AND CULTURE

Research cites many reasons why Industry 4.0 efforts fail. Many of them are of *technical* nature, such as high cost, legacy IT systems, data connectivity, cybersecurity, and so forth. These are all valid, though sometimes outdated, concerns. AI and advanced technologies help to remove these roadblocks. I outlined my arguments for this in-depth in the preceding chapters.

In recent years, the focus shifted to *organizational* challenges. It indeed becomes the focal point of many discussions around Industry 4.0 adoption, especially when the term Digital Transformation is used. Initiatives are critiqued for their focus, mostly on technology and little on transforming the organization.

And I cannot agree more. Technology is *necessary* but *not sufficient*. You need to get people on board and evolve the culture of your organization. Luckily, the AI-fueled flywheel does not only ease technical challenges but also creates an environment in which organizational changes are easier to make.

If you recall the Value Flows of the Industry 4.0 Flywheel, humans are involved at every step along the way. I even made the argument in Section 3.1 that the steps of the flywheel work with purely manual processes. Your people are at the center; they call the shots. AI's role is to empower them to perform higher-value work.

But, of course, there will be resistance to change. New stuff is scary. Employees may fear that AI will render their roles obsolete. And you will face inertia to change culture, especially if you are part of a larger corporation. And all of these fears and challenges are real. Dismissing them will only increase resistance.

The topics of People and Culture and Change Management deserve their own book. Luckily, almost all leadership and management books cover this topic in some depth. And if you are a leader in your organization, you probably already have experience and training around these topics.

I will, hence, focus this chapter on the aspects of People and Culture that interconnect with the flywheel framework; and highlight topics that I believe are often underemphasized in more generalized material around these topics.

6.1   Embrace Agile

By now, you must have noticed that I'm a strong believer in iteration-based methods. Instead of planning out the complete project months and years ahead of time with milestones, create a rough roadmap and work in small iterations – develop, test, receive feedback, repeat.

In fact, small iterations are the core of the flywheel framework. Turning it once is an iteration. Weight is reduced by finding the MVP scope. Once the wheel is spinning, there will be organic adoption.

Agile has a proven record all around the world in all types of projects across all industries. And yes, it also works to change culture and transform even the largest of organizations.

One of the most impressive examples is Kraft Heinz. With USD 27 billion in revenue and over 40,000 employees (2022), it is one of the largest manufacturers in the world.

As part of their multi-year turnaround strategy, Kraft Heinz created a strategy. They call it Agile@Scale to stay current and be able to respond to market changes quicker. [24]

At the center of Agile@Scale are pods. These are groups of 12 people dedicated to solving a specific problem or working on an opportunity. "When I have a pod working on innovation of a specific thing, this is the only thing those 12 people do; they don't do anything else. They are 100% of their time dedicated to fix or to solve that opportunity or that problem," as CEO Miguel Patricio put it.

By the end of 2023, Kraft Heinz has implemented 36 of these pods across all functions of the business and achieved great success, such as increasing the ROI of marketing promotions by 10% through AI. Their goal is to have 10% of their employees dedicated to *transforming* the business while the rest are *running* the business.

The agile pods also allow Kraft Heinz to work with innovative partners and start-ups. They can be included in a pod for some time to collaborate and pilot a technology. By assembling diverse pods and allowing people to switch between *transforming* and *running* the business, the results and insights from these pods make their way back into the day-to-day part of the organization.

Another proof of the value of agile is the work of Andrew McAfee. He found that there are four norms that make some companies exponentially more successful than others. His recent book, *The Geek Way,* describes them in detail.[25] The four norms are: Speed, Science, Ownership, and Openness. Agile encompasses these four norms:

Speed: The world is changing incredibly fast. Instead of having significant changes on a generational scale, there are now disruptive developments multiple times per generation. That imposes a big challenge to companies. They need to keep up and transform themselves to be able to adapt quickly. Speed becomes crucial. And agile is all about speed. Create a light flywheel that you can turn easily. Your organization embraces a culture of creating light, MVP flywheels, allowing them to respond with speed when a new opportunity surfaces.

Science: Each iteration is a small science experiment. Creating a hypothesis (= your plan and work packages for the next iteration), then developing a solution for it, and at the end of the iteration receiving feedback. Did it work, or did it not? How is it received by the customer (internal or external)? Based on this feedback, adjust the plan, and repeat. Agile is going through this cycle every couple of weeks (typically two weeks), while traditional methods might develop in silence for months or even years before they get to test it in the market. Speed enables you to create scientific experiments in weeks.

Ownership: Agile teams (or pods, as Kraft Heinz calls them) are dedicated and have a specific focus. They have clear goals, and most importantly, there are no places to hide. It's a small team where everybody is equal, and everybody can see everyone's progress. Underperformers (intentional or not) have no place to hide. It creates accountability and ownership. There is a sense of belonging.

Openness: While Agile embraces accountability and ownership, it is often used as an example of a self-managing team. Most Agile methods have some form of retrospective included at the end of the iteration. That is a place where the team focuses on the good, the bad, and ideas. They celebrate success, identify things that didn't go well, and brainstorm ideas of what to do differently in the next iteration. It's a continuous cycle of self-improvement. To make this work, it is critical to ensure that you create a place of psychological safety without hierarchies. When there are only good things, chances are high that you do *not* have an amazing team but rather a team that doesn't feel safe to share. And that's a bigger problem than having a team that brings up a lot of bad things[e].

6.2   Choose Bottom-Up over Top-Down

As Paul Hawken puts it, "Real change occurs from the bottom up; it occurs person to person, and it almost always occurs in small groups and locales and then bubbles up and aggregates to larger vectors of change."

Many traditional management techniques focus on top-down, so it is only logical for many Industry 4.0 initiatives to follow this pattern. Especially in manufacturing, people seem to be divided into the "people down there on the shopfloor" and the "management up there." I hope you immediately understand the issues that come with this kind of division. Yes, hierarchy exists for a good reason, and these two groups have different responsibilities, but polarization is never a good thing.

When a group of people comes together, culture will be created one way or the other. It comes from the bottom. New joiners might hear a presentation about the cultural values created by management during onboarding, but once they are on the job, they will adopt whatever culture the surrounding team has.

---

[e] That is, by the way, not exclusive to Agile. Whenever your people only tell you positive news, and it seems that all is going exceptionally fine, chances are you are sitting on a time bomb waiting to explode.

In one of my previous jobs, it took me over a year until I randomly stumbled over a slide deck about the company's culture. Reading through it, I was seriously impressed. It talked about Agile, transparency, accountability, empowerment, and many other values often associated with "modern" management. However, when looking around me, I couldn't see these values reflected in the actions people took. The "top" came up with these values, wrote them down, and somehow hoped (or maybe even believed) that their organization would operate based on these values. As Peter Drucker famously put it, "Culture eats strategy for breakfast."

It's clear that management needs to take an *active* role in creating and changing culture. It should be their number one priority. The difference is *how* they go about it.

Successful changes are *initiated* by management and then strategically seeded across the organization to create the *bottom-up effect*. From the outside, it appears that changes are happening organically bottom-up out of nowhere.

It's similar to how you might go about getting buy-in from your boss. If you make it her or his idea, they are more likely to give it full support; they own it. It might look like it was your boss's idea, but in reality, you *initiated* the change[f].

The same also goes for Industry 4.0 initiatives. Take Kraft Heinz's pods as an example. They dedicate 10% of their

---

[f] Your boss hopefully gives you adequate credit for the idea.

workforce to transform the business and innovate. These 10% will embody the culture of Agile and the norms of speed, science, ownership, and openness. When these people switch back to running the business, they will bring this culture with them. The change is happening bottom-up. The leadership team created the right mechanism and frameworks to change culture by initiating Agile@Scale. The resulting cultural change is not enforced top-down but spreads organically through the people who participated in pods.

6.3   Problem First, Solution Second

The pods from Kraft Heinz are not about implementing a *solution* but about solving a *problem*. Starting with the problem is the very first advice I got when starting MontBlancAI. It's about finding your customers' pain points. What are the things that bother them, and how do you create value by solving those problems?

It's human nature to jump to solutions quickly, but it's important to remain *solution-neutral* until you've really figured out the problem. More often than not, you will find startups that begin with a *solution* and then find the problems their solution can solve. They might find meaningful problems, but they might also end up with a great solution that doesn't have any problems worth solving.

The most promising approach is to start with the problem, and *then* figure out the best solution. The same goes for Industry 4.0. Collecting data, visualizing, and analyzing provides no value by itself if you don't have at least a rough understanding of what the problems are you want to solve.

You might wonder why I bring up this argument in the People and Culture chapter.

Because you will drive the adoption of a solution once it improves the lives of your people. Companies will only work with startups if they make their life easier. Your employees will welcome Industry 4.0 if it solves a problem for *them*. Screening your organization for problems worth solving with Industry 4.0 is critical to driving lasting, bottom-up change.

You can establish a flywheel for each problem (or group them together). Ensure that the person with the problem is part of the team behind the flywheel. They act as the customer, provide feedback to the team after each iteration, and decide what works and what doesn't. If Industry 4.0 ends up solving *their* problem, they will become an advocate and champion the idea. Word will spread organically bottom-up; the wheel will start spinning, and soon, you will end up with an incoming stream of problem suggestions.

Similar to AI, Industry 4.0 can solve many problems, but it cannot solve all of them. It's important not to discourage problem suggestions, but it's equally important to explore multiple solutions first and not use Industry 4.0 (or AI, for that matter) as the default answer. In the end, the bottom line is driven by the fact that the problem is solved, and not what solution is implemented[g].

---

[g] Assuming an equal or negligible cost of implementing the solution.

For situations where Industry 4.0 is indeed the right solution, make sure that you are not creating silos of Industry 4.0 solutions. The power of Industry 4.0 comes when data is connected across many systems. Ensure there is always somebody on the team who keeps the big picture in mind.

6.4   The Team Behind the Flywheel

Jeff Bezos said that no team should be so large that two pizzas can't feed the whole group. The same goes for the team behind a single flywheel. Using the terminology from Kraft Heinz, they can be seen as *pods*. Such a team typically consists of people from these groups:

Agile Coaches: Not always required but especially valuable if the team is inexperienced with Agile. They train people on the Agile method and moderate the process. For example, they ensure feedback sessions during retrospectives are safe spaces.

Business: These are the people that have the *problem*. They can be machine operators from the job floor who observe that the machine has an increased number of stops when a certain product is being produced. They tried a few things to figure out the root cause but without success. Business is the customer of the tech team and provides requirements and domain expertise.

Tech: Developers and engineers that develop the *solution*. They are guided by the businesspeople. They translate often ill-defined requirements into code (if software is the solution). At least one of them needs to have the bigger picture in mind to ensure that the developed solution remains consistent across teams.

Partners: Typically, tech people that bring their solution and help implement it. For many smaller manufacturers, the partners are the main tech team (with support from internal IT). When the partner has a primary SaaS business model, they will naturally ensure that the implemented solution is consistent across teams. Their goal is to create an Industry 4.0 platform solution that works for as many problems as possible.

As I discussed before, it's cheaper than ever to get started with Industry 4.0. The reason is that industry-leading vendors bring the tech solution with them including agile coaching. That removes the skill gap, and you don't need to hire expensive AI developers and agile coaches.

The only, but most important, task left on your plate is to identify a problem and bring it to the table with the people that have it. Remember that the first phase is focused on learning, so keep the problem small and achievable. Of course, the more impactful, the better, but that is not the primary focus during Phase 1. In the second Phase, you can drive impact and monetary ROI.

6.5 Accessible Technology to Democratize

As a natural outcome of bringing the *person with the problem* to the table, the *solution* will be designed to solve their problem. If the solution involves an interface to the user, it is important to understand if this person represents a "typical" user. If not, consider bringing an additional person to the table that represents this group.

Once there is an MVP solution in place, have other people with that problem test the solution and provide feedback. This ensures that the solution is accessible and gives everyone a voice in the process.

The result? You will end up with a solution that people have some ownership in. By repeating this process throughout the organization, you will end up democratizing data and Industry 4.0.

6.6   The Opportunity Cost of Not Changing

Overcoming some of these challenges might seem daunting. It might seem safer to stay put and not invest in Industry 4.0 and AI; and not bother with the associated culture change. However, not taking action is also a decision and one that comes with considerable opportunity cost[h]:

Competitive Disadvantage: Companies that have already embraced Industry 4.0 are seeing substantial improvements in efficiency, productivity, and innovation. These advancements allow them to outperform competitors who are slower to adopt these technologies. By not investing in Industry 4.0, your company risks falling behind, not just in

---

[h] formally defined as "the loss of potential gain from alternative options when a decision is made".

terms of current operations but also in the ability to adapt to future market demands.

Missed Opportunities for Optimization: Industry 4.0 offers unparalleled opportunities for process optimization. From predictive maintenance to optimized resource allocation, the efficiencies gained through AI-fueled Industry 4.0 can lead to significant cost savings and improved output. By not leveraging AI, companies miss out on these optimization opportunities, incurring higher operational costs and lower productivity in comparison to AI-enabled competitors.

Inability to Leverage Data-Driven Decisions: AI's capability to analyze large datasets and provide actionable insights is one of its most powerful features. Companies not investing in AI lose the ability to make informed, data-driven decisions, which can significantly impact strategic planning and day-to-day operations.

Slower Response to Market Changes: The flywheel enhances agility and responsiveness to market trends and customer needs. Companies not incorporating it into their operations may find themselves slower to respond to market changes, leading to missed opportunities and decreased customer satisfaction.

Employee Skill Gap: As Industry 4.0 and AI become more prevalent in the industry, the skills gap for employees trained in these and related technologies widens. Companies not investing in learning (Phase 1) may face challenges in workforce development and might struggle to attract top talent, who often seek employers at the forefront of technology.

Reduced Innovation Potential: Industry 4.0 not only streamlines existing processes but also opens up new avenues for innovation. Companies not investing in AI risk stagnating in terms of product development and may miss out on creating new business models or revenue streams.

Impact on Brand and Reputation: In an era where technological advancement is highly valued, the perception of a company's technological prowess can impact its brand and market reputation. Companies that are seen as technology laggards may find it challenging to maintain their market position.

7

THE ACTION YOU CAN TAKE TODAY

Embarking on the journey of AI-enabled Industry 4.0 integration in your manufacturing processes involves a series of progressive steps. Regardless of your industry, use case, or size, there are fundamental actions that guide you toward harnessing Industry 4.0. While I cannot promise you the ROI of the outcome as there are simply too many variables, I can certainly assure you that you will learn something valuable along the way.

In the preceding chapters, I introduced the AI-fueled Industry 4.0 Flywheel framework on a conceptual level. You might already have made some connections to your own factory and how some of these concepts can be applied. Maybe you already wrote down some notes or even took action.

In this final chapter, my goal is to guide you along the process of identifying *a problem* and then the decision-making around finding a *solution*. Such that by the end of the chapter, you will end up with something tangible that represents your very own MVP version of the flywheel. There will be some boxes for you to write down notes, so I recommend grabbing a pencil before continue reading.

7.1   Find a Problem Worth Solving

It all starts with the problem. But which ones are the ones worth solving? Which ones should be your focus?

The all-time classic *The Goal* from Eliyahu M. Goldratt provides answers. There are two categories of machines:

Bottleneck machines. Bottleneck machines, in a manufacturing process, are like narrow passages that can only handle so much traffic at a time. They limit how much a factory can produce because they work slower than other parts of the production line. The key point here is that these machines not only affect how much can be produced but also how much can eventually be sold. If a bottleneck machine is slow, it doesn't matter how fast the rest of the process is; the overall output is still limited. This means fewer products are available for sale, directly impacting the business's ability to meet market demand and generate revenue. Bottleneck machines constrain the volume of products that can be *sold*.

Non-Bottleneck machines. Non-bottleneck machines, in contrast, have extra capacity and don't hold up the production line. They're the smoother-running parts of the process that can handle more work if needed. While they might not be as critical as the bottlenecks in determining the overall output, they play a vital role in maintaining steady and efficient production. Proper management and scheduling of these machines ensure that they support the bottlenecks effectively and contribute to an uninterrupted and productive manufacturing flow.

Goldratt furthermore argues that there are generally three main goals for a manufacturing plant:

1. Increase Throughput. Increasing throughput means making more products in the same amount of time. It's like a bakery trying to bake more loaves of bread each day without extending its working hours. The goal is to get more finished products out the door, ready to be sold. This doesn't just mean working faster; it's about working smarter to make the whole process more efficient. It's important to keep quality standards high so that an increase in throughput does not result in lower quality but in more products while maintaining quality.

2. Reduce Inventory. Reducing inventory is about having fewer raw materials, works-in-progress, and finished goods sitting around in the factory. Think of it like a kitchen that buys just enough ingredients for a week's meals so nothing goes to waste. By keeping inventory low, the factory saves money and space, and the risk of having unsold products is reduced.

3. Reduce Operating Costs. Reducing operating costs means spending less money to make the products. This could involve finding cheaper suppliers, using less electricity, or making sure machines don't break down as often. It's like a family trying to cut down on household expenses; the goal is to maintain the same lifestyle (or production level) while spending less.

The three goals set for a manufacturing plant, as argued by Goldratt, are directly related to the types of machines involved in the process.

Goals for Bottleneck Machines

For bottleneck machines, the primary aim is to *increase throughput*. This is crucial because every moment these machines are not functioning at their optimal capacity, potential sales are being lost. The focus here is on doing whatever it takes to maximize the output of these critical points in the production line. This includes strategies like reducing unnecessary cleaning, minimizing wait times for materials, streamlining maintenance to prevent downtime, and enhancing the production rate. In essence, every hour saved at a bottleneck machine is an additional hour of producible and sellable products, making the savings in operating costs secondary compared to the gains in sales.

Goals for Non-Bottleneck Machines

On the other hand, non-bottleneck machines, which are not the limiting factor in the production process, require a different approach. The goal for these machines is to *balance the reduction in operating expenses with the costs associated with inventory*. Since these machines already have surplus capacity, saving an hour of their time doesn't translate to increased production like it does with bottleneck machines. Instead, the focus is on actions that can optimize their operation. For example, increasing batch sizes can lead to fewer cleaning cycles, potentially lower personnel costs, and reduced waste, albeit with a need for a larger inventory. Conversely, decreasing batch sizes might increase operational activities but reduce inventory needs.

Identify Bottleneck Machines

When setting goals for manufacturing efficiency, it's crucial to accurately identify bottleneck machines. These are the points in the production line that limit overall output, essentially acting as choke points that slow down the process. Recognizing these bottlenecks is not always straightforward, as they can vary depending on the product being produced and can be obscured by other factors in the production process.

You might already have an intuitive understanding of which machines are the bottlenecks. However, formally mapping out these bottlenecks is a task that requires careful observation and analysis. The bottleneck might shift depending on various factors, including changes in product demand, maintenance schedules, and supply chain dynamics.

To begin identifying these critical machines, start with your best guess based on your knowledge of the production processes. Remember, the goal isn't to be perfect from the outset but to start somewhere and refine your understanding as you gather more data and insights. Here are some strategies to help in identifying bottleneck machines:

Observation of Production Flow. Where in the production line do materials and products tend to accumulate? Is there a specific machine that consistently has a waiting line for materials or products?

Employee Insights. What insights can the production floor staff provide about where delays and issues occur? Are there particular machines or stages in the production process that the staff consistently identify as problematic?

Analysis of Production Data (if available). Which machines have the longest operation times according to our production records? Are there machines that frequently break down or require maintenance, causing production delays?

Here is some space for your notes to identify the bottleneck and non-bottleneck machines for two lines.

Line 1:

_____

My Bottleneck Machine is:

_____

My Non-Bottleneck Machines are:

1.

_____

2.

_____

3.

_____

=====================================

Line 2:

_____

My Bottleneck Machine is:

_____

My Non-Bottleneck Machines are:

1.

_____

2.

_____

3.

_____

Focus on Bottleneck Machines when Operating at Capacity

Once you've identified which machines fall into these categories, the next crucial decision is determining which machine to drill down on further.

Deciding whether to start with a bottleneck or non-bottleneck machine largely hinges on your current demand

and capacity situation. If your demand is high and you're struggling to keep up, indicating that you're operating at or near your capacity limit, then turning your attention to a bottleneck machine is the strategic choice. Improving the efficiency or capacity of a bottleneck machine directly enables you to produce *and* sell more, effectively increasing your bottom line. This is because the bottleneck is the limiting factor in your production capability, and easing this constraint can lead to an immediate increase in throughput.

On the other hand, if demand is not outstripping your production capacity, then focusing on what you've identified as bottleneck machines might not yield significant benefits. In such scenarios, these machines aren't true bottlenecks in the sense that improving them wouldn't lead to an *increase in sales*, as the demand isn't there to absorb the extra production. In fact, enhancing these machines without corresponding demand could inadvertently lead to increased inventory costs, as more products are produced than can be sold.

Therefore, it becomes clear that your initial focus should be on bottleneck machines when demand is high. Any improvement in these areas translates directly into increased production and sales capacity, making them the most impactful points for intervention.

When you are not operating at capacity, there are still plenty of opportunities for improvements. You can cut operating and inventory cost.

Take some notes:

> If I can produce more on Line 1, do I sell more?
> Yes/No
>
> If I can produce more on Line 2, do I sell more?
> Yes/No

If you answered yes to *any* of the above questions, focus on the bottleneck machine of that line. If you answered no to both, then go back to the step before and see if you can't identify another line. If not, no problem, then you don't have a true bottleneck machine as defined by Goldratt. Your focus should be on cutting cost of your non-bottlenecks.

7.1.1   Identify Problems of Your Bottleneck Machine

By now, we have identified a true bottleneck machine. By improving its throughput, it would directly result in increased sales. If you answered yes to both of the questions before, pick the Line with the largest impact.

Let's start by simply writing down what we want to achieve:

> To sell more goods and increase my revenue, I need to increase throughput of the following bottleneck machine:
>
> _____

Sounds simple enough, right?

Unfortunately, in reality, as I'm sure you know better than me, it's not that simple. There is a lot of noise and "buts." In either case, the starting point is understanding what is actually going on, because "If You Can't Measure It, You Can't Improve It."

Measure First

The probing question becomes: Are you able to look up within minutes the percentage of uptime and downtime of your bottleneck machine yesterday? Are you able to drill down into each downtime event and understand what caused it?

If you cannot, then you have you have a measurement problem. Before doing anything, you need to solve that problem. The good news is that the solution to this problem is not complex. It's the first two steps of the flywheel – collect and visualize data. I found it insightful to also write down your and/or your team's intuition about the percentage of downtime. More often than not, the intuition differs from the collected data.

More specifically, you can write down your immediate action:

> To sell more goods and increase my revenue, I need, as a first step, to find a solution to collect and visualize uptime and downtime data and allow drill down into downtime events for my bottleneck machine:
>
> _____
>
> I estimate the avg. percentage of downtime to be: _____ %
>
> My team estimates the avg. percentage to be: ____ %

You might at this stage, put the book aside and get to work. In fact, I encourage you to do that as you just identify a clear *problem worth solving* that results in a light flywheel you can start turning. To read about how to go about finding a solution to this problem, you can jump to Section 7.2.

While having accurate measurements is absolutely *necessary*, it is *not sufficient* to actually increase the throughput of your bottleneck machine.

Identify the Levers

By now, I presume that you have an accurate measurement of the percentage of downtime – either because you already had such a system in place or you just implemented it. Now, we need to identify what levers can be pulled to increase throughput.

It's always a good idea to write it down:

The avg. downtime of my bottleneck machine:

_____

is: _____ %

Because it greatly depends on the specifics of your bottleneck machines what the levers are, I'm not attempting to list them out but give you a *process* that you can follow to identify them yourself and make a *data-driven decision*.

The starting point is the data about downtime and the drilldown into each event. Depending on the solution you implemented, AI and ML might have already turned this data into actionable insights and save you valuable time.

But let's assume for the purpose of this section that you don't have any AI or ML implemented besides your visualization. The goal is then to get your team together and drill down into the data, and understand *which problems* contribute most to your downtime. Such that you can list them out ordered by most to least important.

These are the top five problems that contribute to the downtime of my bottleneck machine:

1.

_____

2.

_____

3.

_____

4.

_____

5.

_____

Note that this is not an easy exercise. More likely than not, it might require going back to the Data Collection step and selecting additional tags you need to monitor. Or, if the data volume is overwhelming and manual analyses are impossible, you are well advised to bring some AI and ML solutions on board.

In either case, the only step left is now the one about acting. You have identified the top problems that will impact your bottom line. Now, it is acting and implementing solutions to the problems that have the highest benefit-to-cost ratio. It might be an Industry 4.0 solution, such as to use ML to predict the breakdown of equipment on the bottleneck machine, but it might also be a mechanical alternation. That is the power of starting with a problem and staying solution-neutral.

Measure Again

Once you have implemented a solution, it is important to measure again and ensure that the solution indeed increased throughput. Everyone involved wants the numbers to look positive. However, it is crucial to discourage tweaking numbers as it creates the wrong incentives.

If the solution increased throughput, you are ready to calculate the monetary ROI and tackle the next problems.

If it didn't, it's still a success as you learned what does *not* work. Go back to identifying the levers with the newly earned knowledge as your understanding has deepened.

In either case, there is another big win here. To get to this stage, you establish a repeatable process by finding a light Flywheel and turning it. You followed the agile methodologically of developing, testing, receiving feedback, and repeating. While the ROI is certainly important, the resulting culture might have an even larger impact in the long run.

7.1.2   Identify Problems of Non-Bottleneck Machines

After focusing on the bottleneck machines in your manufacturing process, attention must also be given to non-bottleneck machines. These machines, which possess excess capacity and do not directly limit your production line's throughput, require a strategic approach to optimize their functionality and contribute to overall efficiency.

Non-bottleneck machines, while not impeding the production flow, play a vital role in the manufacturing ecosystem. They maintain the consistency and steadiness of the production process, supporting bottleneck machines. The goal here is not to increase their output but to optimize their operation in a way that complements the entire production line. This involves balancing operating costs and inventory management to avoid unnecessary expenses and wastage.

Note that the identification of areas of improvement for non-bottleneck machines is more complex than for bottleneck machines. There are more variables at play, and decisions are interconnected between machines. Often, you will face a trade-off between labor, energy, maintenance, and inventory cost. When done right, significant cost savings can be achieved.

Take as an example a robotic packaging system that a large dairy operator in the United States installed in their line. They were having a lot of issues with joint and harness failures. The robot was initially designed to function at a high rate of speed, and then it would sit and wait for product. By slowing down the speed of the robot to match the overall machine capability, they increased the life expectancy of these components eight-fold, which yielded higher throughput, lower operational costs, better quality, and, of course, more reliability. A lot of times, these dimensions go hand in hand. An AI control system could ramp up and down as the overall capacity changes, essentially becoming an adaptive cruise control with lane assist (efficiency and quality control).

While it will heavily depend on your factory's circumstances, I am outlining three common areas for improvements in non-bottleneck machines. Consider them as a starting point from which you can define areas for your own factory.

Machines with high operating cost. Some machinery requires more labor than others. Being able to consolidate the work of two shifts into one shift cuts the labor cost in half (and allows you to allocate these workers to something more valuable, as staff shortage seems to be the norm). It also cuts your utility bill by quite a bit. For non-bottleneck machines, that is a great lever. The approach to identifying such opportunities follows similar steps as for bottleneck machines. Are these machines running as efficiently as possible? Can their energy consumption be reduced, or can their maintenance be scheduled more effectively?

Machines with quality issues. Some steps of the manufacturing process are more challenging and may result in a higher rate of faulty goods. Focus on these does not only improve efficiency but also reduces the waste and cost associated with it. Can changes to non-bottleneck machines reduce waste or lower environmental footprints?

Machines with constant breakdowns. Machines have different reliability. Some run for years without much maintenance, while others require daily care. Unexpected breakdowns of non-bottleneck machines cause distribution in the production flow that could impact the flow of material to our bottleneck machine. Therefore, directly impacting your throughput and the goods you sell. You might have identified such a case in the assessment of your bottleneck machine's downtime and traced it back to a non-bottleneck machine. In these cases, it's critical to be preventive or better predictive about the maintenance of your non-bottleneck machines.

The steps to tackle these opportunities are similar to the ones for bottleneck machines. They follow the same pattern of measurement. Find the levers, act, then measure again.

To illustrate them, let's run with the three areas above – high operating cost, quality issues, and machine breakdowns.

As a starting point and for the purpose of this exercise, identify a non-bottleneck machine for each of the three areas. They can come from the list you created before for the two lines or can be others.

The non-bottleneck machine with the **highest operating cost** is:

_____

The non-bottleneck machine with the **most quality issues** is:

_____

The non-bottleneck machine with the **most breakdowns** is:

_____

Now, let's start by measuring.

Measure First

By picking a non-bottleneck machine for each category, you must either look up the numbers on a dashboard (kudos to you then!), have them memorized, or, more likely, have a gut intuition about it based on your experience.

If you selected based on numbers, great; you are all set and can go to the next section and identify the levers.

If you selected based on your intuition, you need to measure first. While I'm convinced your gut is correct (otherwise, you wouldn't have the position you have). To demonstrate improvement, it's always better to measure and have a number to show.

Now, for the purpose of keeping the following sections concise, let's focus on the first non-bottleneck machine you identified. The one where the operating cost is high[i]. The action then becomes:

To lower my cost, I need, as a first step, to find a solution to collect and visualize operating cost data about personal cost, utility bills, and maintenance cost. That data needs to be tied to throughput and product type.

_____

I estimate the per hour operating cost to be: _____

My team estimates the per hour operating cost to be: _____

As for bottleneck machines, measuring is not sufficient to do something about it. But it will let you identify the levers.

Identify the Levers

Now comes the part you are an expert in. Likely, while collecting the measurements and data, you already identified levers that help you reduce the cost. It could be as straightforward as turning the machine completely off when

---

[i] you can (and should) pick any other non-bottleneck machine. I just chose an example here.

not used, as standby power is substantial for this specific machine. Your utility bill and the environment will thank you for it. It might also be more complex, such as rearranging shift schedules, buying a new, more efficient machine, outsourcing this part of production, or shifting it to a different factory.

Whatever it might be, here is some space for you to take notes:

These are the top five significant contributors to the high operating cost of my non-bottleneck machine:

1.

_____

2.

_____

3.

_____

4.

_____

5.

_____

Now to the final step.

Measure Again

With an Industry 4.0 solution, you are continuously measuring, so measuring again seems natural. It is important, though, to make some sort of report to compare before and after to score the impact of the solution you implemented.

You may have noticed that I kept the description of these steps short as I trust that after reading the section on the bottleneck machines, you got the concept. Also, if you are following the more formal method of Continuous Improvement, then this will sound very familiar to you. The difference is, though, that while following the steps in this book and tying it to Industry 4.0 and AI solutions, you are organically starting your Digital Transformation journey and building out a platform along the way. You are starting to make this Flywheel spin. And it is natural that the first iteration feels painful and slow, don't feel discouraged and trust the process.

Non-Bottleneck Machines are Important

By focusing on non-bottleneck machines, you ensure that every part of your production line is optimized, not just the areas with the most apparent constraints. This comprehensive approach can lead to significant savings and efficiency improvements, contributing positively to the bottom line. In essence, while non-bottleneck machines may not dictate the pace of production, their optimized operation is essential for a lean, cost-effective, and environmentally sustainable manufacturing process.

7.1.3   Problems of a Line: Risk and Quality Control

In addition to Eliyahu M. Goldratt's insights, another critical aspect of managing a manufacturing line is ensuring risk and quality control. This aspect functions as a constraint where the manufacturing process must meet specific quality standards. These standards can be set internally, mandated by regulators, or demanded by customers. Failing to meet these standards can put the brand at significant risk, potentially leading to reputational damage and financial loss.

Industry 4.0 technologies play a pivotal role in this context. They offer the capability to learn the normal behavior of a process (prediction) and identify any deviations that might indicate a quality concern (detection).

Consider the example of tank cleaning, which must adhere to regulatory standards such as maintaining a temperature of 80 degrees Celsius for 10 minutes. An Industry 4.0 system can verify compliance with these requirements and facilitate root cause analysis if deviations occur.

While some quality thresholds are rigid, like regulatory requirements, others are more flexible and akin to cooking guidelines – there's always a range. In complex manufacturing processes with thousands of parameters, manually setting and adjusting these thresholds is impractical and unscalable. Machine learning (ML) can be instrumental here, as it learns and adapts to these ranges automatically, ensuring optimal product quality and consistency.

Issues related to quality control often emerge not just at the shop floor level but are a significant concern for Quality

Assurance (QA) and Quality Control (QC) departments. Unlike problems that are isolated to a single machine, quality control issues often require monitoring and tracking across the entire production line. This is where concepts like Batch Tracing or Track and Trace systems become essential. These systems enable manufacturers to monitor the entire lifecycle of a product, from raw materials to finished goods, ensuring traceability and accountability at every stage of the manufacturing process.

By integrating Industry 4.0 solutions for risk and quality control, manufacturers can enhance their ability to maintain high-quality standards, comply with regulatory requirements, and reduce the risk of quality failures. This proactive approach to quality management not only safeguards the brand reputation but also optimizes the manufacturing process, making it more efficient, reliable, and customer-centric.

7.2   The Process of Finding a Solution

In the evolving world of manufacturing, particularly under the umbrella of Industry 4.0, finding the right solution to a challenge involves a crucial decision between in-house development and external vendor collaboration. This choice, central to the effectiveness, cost, and timeline of solution implementation, requires a comprehensive and balanced approach.

The first step is to define the problem clearly, whether it's related to operational efficiency, cost reduction, quality control, or risk management. With a well-defined problem, the next critical step is to remain solution-neutral initially, carefully considering the trade-offs between developing a solution in-house and seeking external vendor expertise. This neutrality is key in ensuring that the final decision is based on objective analysis rather than preconceived preferences.

Gathering and analyzing data is a pivotal step, crucial for both in-house and external solutions. It involves collecting relevant production metrics, machine performance data, and quality control reports. Here, in-house teams often have the advantage of intimate process knowledge, while external vendors bring broader industry insights and plug-and-play solutions and may offer innovative perspectives that are not immediately apparent internally.

The ideation of solutions should consider the strengths and limitations of both approaches. In-house development offers more control and can be closely aligned with specific organizational needs. However, it may require significant investment in new skills and technology. On the other hand, external vendors can provide scalable, technologically advanced solutions that are usually more cost-effective.

Evaluating the feasibility, cost, and long-term implications of each option is crucial. In-house projects might lead to higher initial costs due to the need for skill development and technological investment. Vendor solutions, however, often come with more predictable costs and can include ongoing support and maintenance, making them a more appealing choice in many scenarios.

Pilot testing is essential, whether the development is in-house or through a vendor. This step ensures that the solution is effective and integrates well with existing processes. Vendors often excel in this area, offering well-tested solutions and expertise in implementation, reducing the risk of costly errors or disruptions.

Training and support are also critical considerations. In-house solutions may require a substantial training effort, whereas vendors typically include this as part of their service, along with ongoing support. This aspect can be particularly advantageous for vendors, as it ensures continuous improvement and adaptation of the solution to changing needs.

Continuous monitoring and iterative improvement are key, irrespective of the development approach. Collect feedback, monitor performance metrics, and be prepared to make necessary adjustments. In a dynamic sector like manufacturing, the ability to adapt and evolve with changing needs and technologies is crucial.

In conclusion, while both in-house and vendor developments have their merits, the trend leans towards vendor solutions as a more viable option for many manufacturers. Vendors often provide a combination of technological innovation, scalability, and ongoing support that can be challenging to replicate in-house. By staying solution-neutral initially and carefully analyzing the trade-offs, manufacturers can make a decision that aligns with their strategic objectives, operational needs, and long-term vision, often finding that vendor collaborations offer the most advantageous path forward.

7.3 Scorecard and Closing

You might find it contradicting that I left space in a book to write notes on *paper* (if you have a physical copy in front of you) while trying to make the case for digitalization. And believe it or not, I'm still a fan of the physical book. Turning pages feels like progress to me, and it allows me to focus.

Whether you made notes in the Sections before or just read through them, at MontBlancAI we developed a digital version of it. It comes in the form of a free scorecard that consists of a couple of questions similar to the ones in this Chapter. It only takes a couple of minutes to complete, and you will receive a customized report with tailored recommendations for actions you can take.

To access this free scorecard, simply scan the QR code here:

QR Code 3: free scorecard assessment

I hope this book has served as both a helpful guide and a thought-provoking read. It's entirely normal if you find yourself disagreeing with certain parts; in fact, my aim is to challenge the status quo and provoke critical thinking. And remember, as mentioned in the introduction, should this book not deliver the value you expected, please feel free to contact me for a refund of your purchase price.

In closing, I leave you with this reflection:

AI will not replace humans.

But Manufacturers embracing AI will replace those that don't.

Which side of the coin will you be on?

ACKNOWLEDGMENT

In the creation of "Artificial Intelligence WILL Revolutionize Manufacturing", I have had the privilege of collaborating with numerous individuals whose knowledge and enthusiasm have been invaluable. While I choose not to list names, as such a list is never complete and I would inevitably miss someone, each of you who has contributed knows the role you've played. I am deeply grateful for your input and support.

Your insights and experiences have enriched the content of this book significantly. Your perspectives and expertise have not only informed but also inspired my writing.

To my colleagues, friends, and the many professionals in the manufacturing and AI sectors whom I've encountered, your support, encouragement, and dedication have been immensely influential and appreciated.

This book is a testament to the collective wisdom and contributions of all those with whom I've had the honor of interacting.

Thank you for your part in this journey.

- Markus

ENDNOTES

i McKinsey & Company. "The economic potential of generative AI: The next productivity frontier." June 14, 2023. https://www.mckinsey.com/capabilities/mckinsey-digital/our-insights/the-economic-potential-of-generative-ai-the-next-productivity-frontier

ii McKinsey & Company. "The state of AI in 2023: Generative AI's breakout year." August 1, 2023. https://www.mckinsey.com/capabilities/quantumblack/our-insights/the-state-of-ai-in-2023-generative-ais-breakout-year

---

[1] "Search in the Land of Information Silos." Galaxy Consulting Blog. December 31, 2016. https://galaxyconsulting.weebly.com/blog/archives/12-2016.

[2] "What is Industrie 4.0?" Plattform Industrie 4.0. Accessed January 13, 2024. https://www.plattform-i40.de/IP/Navigation/EN/Industrie40/WhatIsIndustrie40/what-is-industrie40.html.

[3] Kushmaro, Philip. "5 Ways Industrial AI is Revolutionizing Manufacturing." CIO, September 27, 2018. https://www.cio.com/article/222332/5-ways-industrial-ai-is-revolutionizing-manufacturing.html.

[4] Charalambous, Eleftherios, Robert Feldmann, Gérard Richter, and Christoph Schmitz. "AI in Production: A Game Changer for Manufacturers with Heavy Assets." McKinsey & Company, March 7, 2019. https://www.mckinsey.com/capabilities/quantumblack/our-insights/ai-in-production-a-game-changer-for-manufacturers-with-heavy-assets.

[5] "Artificial Intelligence (AI) is Just Getting Started Revolutionizing Manufacturing." Smart Industry, August 22, 2023. https://www.smartindustry.com/artificial-intelligence/article/33010172/artificial-intelligence-ai-is-just-getting-started-revolutionizing-manufacturing.

[6] "How AI Builds A Better Manufacturing Process." Forbes. July 17, 2018. https://www.forbes.com/sites/insights-intelai/2018/07/17/how-ai-builds-a-better-manufacturing-process/?sh=733e731f1e84.

[7] Mitchell, Robert. "How AI is Changing Manufacturing: Revolutionizing Efficiency & Growth." WSI, July 3, 2023. https://www.wsiworld.com/blog/how-ai-is-changing-manufacturing-revolutionizing-efficiency-growth.

[8] Sandler, Arkady. "How AI is Changing the Manufacturing Industry." Unite.AI. May 6, 2023. https://www.unite.ai/how-ai-is-changing-the-manufacturing-industry/.

[9] Maoulida, Naguib. "How AI is Redefining the Manufacturing Industry." Ivy Partners. May 22, 2023. https://www.ivy.partners/how-ai-is-redefining-the-manufacturing-industry/.

[10] "How is AI revolutionizing Manufacturing?" Korcomptenz. Accessed [Access Date]. https://www.korcomptenz.com/blog/how-is-ai-revolutionizing-manufacturing/.

[11] Cravotta, Nicholas. "How AI is Revolutionizing Industrial Manufacturing." Association for Advancing Automation, August 18, 2022. https://www.automate.org/industry-insights/how-ai-is-revolutionizing-industrial-manufacturing.

[12] Gander, Patti. "Revolutionizing Manufacturing: How AI is Transforming the Industry." AssuredPartners, October 5, 2023. https://www.assuredpartners.com/blogs/manufacturing/2023/revolutionizing-manufacturing-how-ai-is-transforming-the-industry/.

[13] Moore, Lindsay. "10 AI use cases in manufacturing." TechTarget, October 10, 2023. https://www.techtarget.com/searcherp/feature/10-AI-use-cases-in-manufacturing.

[14] Torrence, Carl. "Top 11 case studies of artificial intelligence in manufacturing." InData Labs. October 10, 2023. https://indatalabs.com/blog/ai-use-cases-in-manufacturing.

[15] "The Evolution of AI in Manufacturing." Eide Bailly, November 2023. https://www.eidebailly.com/insights/articles/2023/11/the-evolution-of-ai-in-manufacturing.

[16] "Oyak Cement." AVEVA. Accessed January 6, 2024. https://www.aveva.com/en/perspectives/success-stories/oyak-cement/.

[17] Votorantim Cimentos. "Votorantim Cimentos transforms operations in its first year with AVEVA." Customer case study. Last modified September 2021. https://www.aveva.com/content/dam/aveva/documents/perspectives/success-stories/SuccessStory_AVEVA_Votorantim_09-21.pdf.coredownload.inline.pdf.

[18] New Belgium Brewing Co. "New Belgium Brewing Improves Performance and Meets Customer Demands." Customer case study. Last modified June 2020. https://www.aveva.com/content/dam/aveva/documents/perspectives/success-stories/new-belgium-brewing-co-06-20.pdf.coredownload.inline.pdf.

[19] "The Business Case for Digital Transformation." White paper. Last modified February 2023. https://www.aveva.com/content/dam/aveva/documents/white-papers/WhitePaper_AVEVA_BusinessCaseDigitalTransformation_23-02.pdf.coredownload.inline.pdf.

[20] "Henkel harnesses its big data to drive sustainability and boost energy efficiency." Klinkmann. Accessed January 6, 2024. https://www.klinkmann.lv/henkel-harnesses-its-big-data-to-drive-sustainability-and-boost-energy-efficiency/.

[21] "Accessible Anywhere: How Pfizer Deployed The PI System To Enable Production Analysis Across The Organization." Pharmaceutical Online. Accessed January 6, 2024. https://www.pharmaceuticalonline.com/doc/accessible-anywhere-how-pfizer-deployed-the-pi-system-to-enable-production-analysis-across-the-organization-0001.

[22] Mengqi, Xu, and Ding Yi. "Wuxi Factory Embraces New Technologies for Smarter Production." CGTN, September 19, 2018. https://news.cgtn.com/news/3d3d674d336b6a4d7a457a6333566d54/share_p.html.

[23] Goldratt, Eliyahu M. "The Goal: A Process of Ongoing Improvement." Great Barrington, MA: North River Press, 1992.

[24] "The Kraft Heinz Company - Kraft Heinz Outlines the Next Phase of Its Transformation at the 2022 CAGNY Conference." The Kraft Heinz Company. February 22, 2022. https://news.kraftheinzcompany.com/press-releases-details/2022/Kraft-Heinz-Outlines-the-Next-Phase-of-Its-Transformation-at-the-2022-CAGNY-Conference/default.aspx.

[25] McAfee, Andrew. "The Geek Way: The Radical Mindset that Drives Extraordinary Results." Hardcover Edition. New York: [Publisher Name], November 14, 2023.

Made in the USA
Columbia, SC
12 February 2025

53728540R00083